SPANISH UNDERGROUND DRAMA

GEORGE E. WELLWARTH **SPANISH UNDERGROUND DRAMA**

The Pennsylvania State
University Press

University Park and London

Library of Congress Catalog Card No. 76-39288
International Standard Book Number 0-271-01154-8
Printed in the United States of America
Designed by Larry Krezo

Library of Congress Cataloging in Publication Data
Wellwarth, George E   1932–
    Spanish underground drama.
    Includes bibliographical references.
    1. Spanish drama—20th century—History and
criticism. 2. Underground literature—Spain.
I. Title.
PQ6115.W4   862'.6'409   76-39288
ISBN 0-271-01154-8

For Napier Wilt

". . . ferocissimi per acies aut proscriptione cecidissent, ceteri nobilium, quanto quis servitio promptior, opibus et honoribus extollerentur ac novis ex rebus aucti, tuta et praesentia quam vetera et periculosa mallent."

Tacitus, *Annals*, Bk. I, Ch. 2.

"La vraie trahison est de suivre le monde comme il va, et d'employer l'esprit à le justifier."

Jean Guéhenno, *Caliban parle*.

CONTENTS

PREFACE

The late Robert Capa, who made his reputation as a photographer during the Spanish Civil War, lived the paradox of being a pacifist war photographer. When asked what he would most like to be, he replied, "Unemployed." Similarly, if asked what I would most like this book on contemporary Spanish underground drama to become, I would reply, "Out of date." The plays discussed in the book will never become out of date, for they are far too good—some of them, I believe, are among the few authentic works of genius that the theater possesses—to be tied to the fluctuations of taste and of time. My hope is simply that the rubric "underground" will become out of date rapidly, and that these playwrights will be recognized and produced openly.

This book is in every conceivable sense introductory. My principal purpose in writing it is to acquaint students of Spanish drama with the existence of an extensive and artistically interesting theater movement in contemporary Spain. This movement I have called the "Spanish underground drama," because, for the most part it remains unproduced and unpublished in Spain as a result of the restrictions imposed on it by the censors. Most of the plays discussed in the book exist, as yet, only in manuscript form, and one of my purposes in writing it has been to stimulate other researchers to further investigation. This book is by no means an exhaustive study of the movement. Not only are there many worthy plays that I have not commented on, but there are younger authors of great promise, such as Vicente Romero, just beginning to write. There is, in other words, a definite need for more studies in this field.

Since the primary purpose of this book is to introduce its readers to the truly "underground" authors, I have omitted works by writers such as Antonio Buero-Vallejo, Alfonso Sastre, Carlos Muñiz, and Lauro Olmo, who clearly belong to the movement, but who are already, to some extent, known to the English-speaking world as a result of scholarly studies and text editions.[1]

Perhaps a word is in order explaining how this book came to be written at all, since it is almost a paradigm of scholarly serendipity. Late in 1964, shortly after the first edition of my book *The Theatre of Protest and Paradox* was published in England, I received a letter from José Maria Bellido, of whom I had never heard, saying that he had read the book during a recent trip to England, had liked it very much as far as it went, but that he was extremely disappointed to see that I wrote about current English, American, French, and German drama while completely ignoring Spanish drama. I replied by explaining that current Spanish drama had not been included because, first, I didn't know there was any and, second, I didn't know a word of Spanish. Sr. Bellido thereupon invited my wife and myself to visit him at his home in San Sebastián and he sent me a copy of one of his plays translated into English by the British playwright David Turner. The play was *Football* (subsequently published in Michael Benedikt and George E. Wellwarth, eds., *Modern Spanish Theatre* (New York: E. P. Dutton & Co., 1968, pp. 329–416). I decided then and there that if it was indeed representative of the sort of drama currently being written in Spain, the sooner I learned Spanish the better. Soon thereafter we visited Sr. Bellido and were introduced by him to José Monleón, editor of *Primer Acto*. Sr. Monleón asked me to write some articles on the current American theater for his journal and also advised me to go to Toledo to look up a talented, but as yet totally unknown, playwright there named Antonio Martínez Ballesteros. After I had written some articles for *Primer Acto*, José Ruibal and other playwrights got in touch with me and asked me to read their plays. The plays that were sent to me were of a literary and theatrical quality that deserved a better fate than that to which they had hitherto been condemned. In the spring of 1970, aided by a grant from the American Philosophical Society, I went once more to Spain and collected well over one hundred manuscripts from the playwrights discussed in this book.

PREFACE

A word of explanation about the typographical style used for the titles of the plays: Spanish titles are in italics, and are followed by an English translation in parentheses. If the play has been published in English, the English title is in italics also, and the play is referred to in the text by that English title. If the play has not been published in English, I have translated its title, which appears in quotes after the introduction of the title, but the play is subsequently referred to by its Spanish title.

I would like to express my gratitude for the courtesies shown to me in Spain by the directors of the Teatro Español, the Ateneo de Madrid, and the Casas de Cultura of Toledo and Talavera de la Reina, who invited me to lecture on the new Spanish drama and other subjects. Thanks are due to the New York University Press for permission to reprint some passages from my *The Theatre of Protest and Paradox*, revised edition. Thanks are also due to the American Philosophical Society and the Research Foundation of the State University of New York for grants that materially aided the completion of this study. My wife Marcia was of great assistance to me as an interpreter in the early stages of this study and has since suffered through its writing. I would like to emphasize that the opinions expressed in this book, as well as the interpretations of the plays, are entirely my own and were arrived at in complete independence of the authors, who are in no way responsible for them.

NOTES

1. For an account of Buero-Vallejo, Sastre, and Muñiz see the chapter on the Spanish drama in my *The Theatre of Protest and Paradox*, rev. ed. (New York: New York University Press, 1971), pp. 353–384. Lauro Olmo's one-act play *La noticia* was published as *The News Item* together with a brief introduction in Michael Benedikt and George E. Wellwarth, eds., *Modern Spanish Theatre* (New York: E. P. Dutton & Co., 1968), pp. 319–327.

1

"LIGHT ON THE UNDERGROUND"

"Underground drama" is merely a somewhat provocative and intriguing name for a literary phenomenon that is all too common: censored drama. The repression of literature, dramatic or otherwise, is a tradition honored by time and use, if by nothing else; and it is practiced in most countries throughout the world today. Whenever a dictatorial government comes into power, one of its first acts is the institution of censorship. There are several reasons for this. A dictatorial government may be defined as one that does not base its actions on the possibility of its peaceful replacement by its opposition. The opposition must consequently be eliminated, repressed, or converted into amiable marionettes, depending upon the extent of the government's commitment to its position of power, i.e., depending upon its unscrupulousness. From this it follows that the members and active supporters of such a government are absolutely convinced of the rectitude of their principles and actions, their minds closed to the possibility of any alternatives. People who have closed minds and are absolutely convinced of their own rectitude are mental perverts, intellectuals *manqués*; those who accept their principles and support their actions on faith are retarded in their anthropological development, obsessed with a primal urge to reverse the uncomfortable and disturbing process of evolution and go from human reason back to animal instinct. No one fears free thought more than those who have rejected it, usually from fear of the responsibilities it brings, and those who are incapable of understanding it. Hence the

1

institution of censorship almost as a reflex action by dictatorial governments as soon as they assume power. Fulminations against the idiocy and inevitable inefficacy of censorship are useless: the persons to whom they are addressed do not read and/or cannot understand them. The last word on the subject was, after all, said by Milton in his "Areopagitica," but Milton, like so many polemicists for freedom, is fated to be read and understood only by those who already agree with him. Indeed, the persuasive ability of literature is so suspect that the urge to censor, which is so rampant among the unlettered, must be classified as paranoid. We have seen this unhappily repetitive syndrome most recently in Greece and Brazil, where, as usual, mental bestiality is cloaked with unctuous expressions of moral reform and insouciant assumptions of moral omniscience.

The theater is always in a more precarious position than the rest of literature when power is assumed by rhetoricians whose reading has never penetrated beyond the comic book level. This is natural enough, since the theater is the most immediate of the arts. Theater speaks directly and makes its effect instantly and spontaneously or not at all. It exemplifies the paradox of being at once the most profound and most complex of the arts and of being able to reach the least literate segments of the populace. No preparation is required for the theater: the groundling and the intellectual may find different things in the play, but each can find something according to his kind. It is undeniable that the awareness of these facts has led dramatists at various times to use the stage as a hortatory instrument. It is equally undeniable that—very rarely—this use has been effective. And from this has sprung the blind fear of subversion as make-believe that paralyzes the "minds" of the world's Ministers of Culture and/or Propaganda. Parkinson's Law, to be sure, may be at work here too: ever more plays must be censored in order to display the necessity of censors. The peculiar discrimination to which the theater is subject with regard to censorship can be seen in contemporary Portugal, where theater is censored but printed books are not. (Because Portugal has the lowest literacy rate in Western Europe, books do not pose a threat.)

The situation in present-day Spain is typical of censorship as an institution. No precise rules are laid down. The administration of the censorship is purely arbitrary and willful. This vagueness is a necessary characteristic of the institution because the inbred paranoia of the censorial mind makes it constantly fearful of the appearance of new forms of literary "subversion." The law must consequently be kept open to deal with unforseen contingencies. As a result of this "open" policy, the author in Spain today never knows in advance what reception his work will meet with from the censor. Under Britain's anachronistic and comparatively laughable censorship (since no one took it seriously and it could be openly and easily subverted) the authors knew where they were: as long as they did not insult or put on the stage any reigning Heads of State and as long as they looked upon sex as the *stoff* of dirty jokes and not as something involving serious problems and as long as they did not blaspheme against God or the Archbishop of Canterbury, they could arrange to sell tickets to their plays on the open market instead of in the form of club membership cards. In Spain today, on the other hand, the author is like a man trapped in an elevator: he never knows whether he will be going up or down next, nor how long he will stop when he gets there; furthermore, the elevator is dark so he cannot see the numbers on the floors, which are probably unnumbered anyway.

Censorship of the theater in post Civil War Spain has been marked all along by this unpredictable attitude. Some sort of low point of idiocy was reached during the stultifying regime of Gabriel Arias Salgado, who is reported to have said that as a result of the censorship of the theater 80 per cent more Spanish souls are entering Heaven. Arias's mule-headed doctrinaire approach was followed by the cynical pragmatism of Manuel Fraga Iribarne, who in turn was followed by the more narrow-minded Sánchez Bella. Frequently apparent relaxations of the censorship rules turn out on closer examination to be nothing of the sort, an example being the recent decree abolishing pre-censorship. While this may sound like a liberalization —publishers and producers are no longer required to submit their texts to the censors before making them public—it is in effect a tightening of the system, since under the consequent post-censorship a publisher may have his whole edition confiscated after he has gone to the expense of printing it, or a producer may have his play banned after he has gone to the expense of rehearsing it. The result, obviously, is that publishers and producers are reluctant to have anything to do with a work unless it is blatantly safe.[1]

This explains the large number of unpublished and unproduced plays by the better Spanish authors, who thus become, *faute de mieux*, underground authors. It is not at all unusual for an author to write a play and then wait three years for a noncommercial production by the students of a private theatre school, an experience recorded by Ramón Gil Novales.[2] He was, indeed, particularly lucky. The three year time lag between writing and production is comparatively short for Spain. Although the noncommercial production brought the author no money, the play was performed by the Adriá Gual School of Drama of Barcelona, certainly one of the best theater schools in the world today, thanks largely to its director, Ricard Salvat, one of Europe's leading theater directors and scholars. At this point it might be argued that a three year time lag between writing and production is not unusual in the United States either. Economic censorship can be just as inhibiting as political censorship. This is very true, but there is a qualitative difference. Economic censorship is an essentially empty threat. It can be circumvented either with money or with noncommercial productions such as the off-off-Broadway storefront theatres and the academic theatres. That the academic theatres in the United States are grievously falling down on the job and shirking their responsibility to the original drama, both native and foreign, is another matter. In any case, the effect of economic censorship and the failure of academic theatres to combat it is already becoming evident in the extraordinary paucity of new American plays. There is an inward turning spiral leading eventually to nothingness here: the less opportunity for plays to be produced, the less plays written and so on *ad nihil*. When Shaw said that Dickens was the greatest English playwright since Henry Fielding, who did not write for the stage, he was not speaking idly but uttering a profound and hitherto immutable theatrical truth: that playwriting diminishes in direct proportion to opportunity of production. Spain is the exception. I do not want to belabor the point made by all other writers of books on Spain that Spain is different, unique, mysterious, exotic; that it has an ethos and a mystique all its own; that Spain, cut off from Europe by the Pyrenees, has by some perverse process of geographic agglutination become a peninsula of the Dark Continent. Indeed I think none of this is true. The Spaniard is both culturally and socially very much part of the European community, his "peculiarities" being largely wished on him by romantic "analysts" beguiled by bullfights, flamenco, and the strangeness of Moorish architecture. Nonetheless, there is a distinctively Spanish quality, and that is a stubbornness so strong that it overrides material considerations. Stubbornness in this sense is a wholly admirable

4

quality, as is the devotion to abstract ideals that is its foundation. And it is in this quality that the cause of the extraordinary efflorescence of contemporary Spanish drama must be sought. Contemporary Spanish underground drama is not completely underground. It is underground the way an iceberg is undersea: a small part of it shows in the form of occasional licensed publications and even more occasional licensed one-night productions. One-night productions are a peculiarly Machiavellian invention of the censors, who, having no principles, are nothing if not pragmatic (a very international characteristic). The theory is that the extremely limited number of people who could attend a single performance are not enough to worry about. Furthermore, not even isolated conversions to undesirable points of view would take place, since the audience at such a performance would consist of enthusiasts—that is, of the already-converted—who can, of course, also be usefully observed by the secret police.

Thus the situation in Spain today is effectively the same, though qualitatively different, as the situation in the United States: political censorship causes as definite a spiral of diminishing returns in the production of drama as does economic censorship. The hit plays in Madrid and Barcelona, the only cities in Spain with active professional theaters, are like the hit plays of Broadway—often they are the hit plays of Broadway—and good plays (i.e., controversial plays, plays of ideas) are by definition excluded from the theater. The qualitative differences lie in the fact that the theater in the United States *is* free (i.e., any play can be produced if the money can be found or if the university theater director has enough courage), and in the fact that Spanish authors refuse to be discouraged and stubbornly go on turning out good play after good play. Bread is cast upon the unresponsive waters with a prodigality that is as amazing as it is admirable.

At this point it might be well to look into the historical causes of this unfortunate situation. The immediate cause, of course, was the Civil War which ravaged the country and its people so thoroughly between 1936 and 1939, that for years afterward a spirit of savage repression ruled the victors to the exclusion of almost everything else and a spirit of hopeless lassitude engulfed the defeated. The Civil War itself, however, must be seen in its proper historical perspective. It was by no means the sudden cataclysmic outburst that it appeared to be to foreigners unfamiliar with Spanish history. It

5

was, rather, the not at all unexpected culmination of a series of civil wars that had been building up for two hundred years. During those two centuries there were very few years indeed in which Spain was free from internecine strife. The factions that fought in the Civil War had been fighting under one name or another ever since the eighteenth century, a fact that serves partially to explain the extraordinary savagery and single-mindedness—extraordinary even for a civil war—that characterized the Spanish conflict. The thousands of foreigners who went to Spain to fight for either side, went under the impression that they were fighting for contemporary issues, but, unknown to them, they were being absorbed into the mainstream of Spanish history which had unfolded over the previous two hundred years and more.

The series of conflicts which culminated in the Civil War can probably be traced back to the schism between liberals and conservatives created by Aranda's anti-clericalism in the late 1760's. During the conflicts of the following century and more this schism was frequently blurred by the fact that whether a Spaniard was a liberal or a conservative, a proclerical or an anticlerical, a believer in spiritual values or a believer in materialistic values, he was always first and foremost an absolutist. Only a few intellectuals—none of them ever a national leader—were able to rise above this absolutism. Not the least significant fact about the new Spanish drama, indeed, is that its writers are among Spain's first philosophical relativists. Absolutism was reflected in the intensity with which the many conflicts were fought and the callousness with which the vanquished were invariably treated. Not only was the peculiar ferocity of the Civil War nothing new, having been matched in miniature by the Carlist wars, but the infantile aberrations of Falangism were nothing new either. Falangism is the Spanish form of Fascism, which may be defined as the abrogation of personal responsibility and the fetishistic worship of slavishness. It is epitomized in the Spanish Foreign Legion's mystic devotion to death, which bears an intriguing similarity to the Japanese *kamikaze* mystique, and in the almost unbelievable slogan "Long live death!" which its founder, General Millán Astray, was fond of roaring out whenever nothing more sensible occurred to him. In a similar frenzy of mindlessness the inhabitants of Madrid welcomed Ferdinand VII back to the throne in 1814 with cries of "Death to Liberty!" The Civil War, then, was not a sudden outbreak or a unique high point in Spanish history. It was the culmination of a long and complex series of events, and, temporarily at least, it halted Spanish history. Franco billed himself as the liberator of Spain and the restorer of its honor and its traditions. There can be little doubt that, ignoring the grotesque unsuitability of his appearance for the role, he saw himself as a second Cid come to drive the political infidel out of the land as the first had driven the religious infidel out. Ironically, Franco performed his second *Reconquista* with the indispensable aid of those very religious infidels that the Cid had driven out—their first return, though in sadly degenerated form, to the country whose culture they had done so much to form.

After the civil war, Spain was as if chloroformed. And, indeed, after the horrors of that war a period of suspended animation was very much in order. The victors spent the ensuing years rebuilding the hierarchical pyramid of privilege that had been threatened by the egalitarian ideals of the Republic. The pyramid once more reconstructed with all the weight sucked up to the narrow part and the broad base on which it rested squeezed dry, with glowing crucifixes incongruously perched upon the top as if to bless the crowded burial chambers within, the builders felt they could once more drift into reactionary somnolence while savoring incense-flavored dreams of their superiority. Nothing epitomizes this attitude so much as the monument of the Valley of the Fallen in the Sierra to the northwest of Madrid. This enormous structure consists of a church cut into the mountain and capped by a cross of truly grandiose proportions. Its expressed purpose was to reunite the nation by serving as a monument and burial place for the fallen of both sides. It was built by the forced labor of Republican prisoners on the "Arbeit macht frei" principle, thus adding a few more to the fallen of at least one side. Its basic design principle seems to be that massiveness is a sign of infinite compassion. In the chapel at the side of the dome, reportedly bigger than that of St. Peter's, there is a cross over the door of the sacristy with the enigmatic inscription, "Caídos por Dios y por España, 1936–1939. RIP." The educated Spanish reader, who has been well described as a man who gets all his information by reading between the lines, may find much to exercise his faculties here. The enormous nave, also bigger than that of St. Peter's, gives one the feeling of being in a Moscow subway station, and leads one to brood over the curious attraction hollow massiveness has for totalitarian architects. In sum, the monument, like the thing it symbolizes, is a failure. The beautiful mountainside has become another casualty of the Civil War. The monument "for the fallen of both sides," built by the defeated as a penance imposed by their Pharaonic conquerors, makes the mountainside look as if it had a grisly skin disease, with the enormous cross surmounting it like a great suppurating and erupting cyst. A more accurate view of the monument's "reconciling" effect is that given by Fernando Díaz-Plaja when he points out that it required "an expenditure of men, money, and material which would have sufficed to put a roof over the head of every Spaniard whom the fortunes of war had unhoused."[3]

The first fifteen or twenty years after the end of the Civil War was a period, initially, of revenge rather than reconciliation. Later, it was one of smug complacency as the winners sat firmly on the losers and contemplated the rest of Europe crumbling in the grip of the war for which their rebellion had been the rehearsal. The most trenchant summing up of this period was the Abbot of Montserrat's when he contradicted Franco's claim of having given Spain twenty-five years of peace by saying that they had been twenty-five years of victory for Franco, not peace for Spaniards, and that the victors had never let the losers forget who won.[4] This attitude naturally led to the state of apathy that characterized the bulk of the populace during those years. The country was as if in a stupor, each person who was not favored with some of the spoils of victory concentrated morbidly inward upon himself, contemplating his hunger (much of Spain was in a state of semistarvation during those years), and pondering with a resentment dulled by hopelessness "this world, which, alas, [had] not been all it might have been, this world in which everything [had] gone wrong bit by bit though no one [could] ever quite understand why."[5] Cela speaks also of the people in his microcosmic café or "hive" as believing "that things happen as they do because they happen, and that it is never worthwhile to put anything right."[6] But, again, we must remember that this attitude was nothing new. Just as the Civil War itself had been only an intensification and destructive coda to the internal struggles that had been rending and polarizing Spain for more than two hundred years, so the post Civil War apathy was only an intensification of the brooding lulls, at once exhausted and preparatory, which had separated those struggles for anachronistic and illusory ideals. As Ortega y Gasset put it, the history of Spain for the last three hundred years was "a long coma of egotism and idiocy."[7] The result was, though Ortega may have been a bit premature in the extremity of his self-lacerating pessimism, that Spaniards had become "not so much a people as a cloud of dust that was left hovering in the air when a great people went galloping down the high road of history."[8]

One of the things that contributed to the transformation of a great people into a cloud of dust after the Civil War was the new censorship. Another more debatable one was the self-doubting introspection that Salvador de Madariaga called a characteristic of Spanish psychology—"the tendency to give up all interest and to withdraw within the tent of silence and passivity when actions and words are useless." An example of this was "the wholesale inhibition of the Spanish political intelligentsia under the Primo de Rivera dictatorship."[9] This inhibition was, of course, repeated under Franco's dictatorship, though Madariaga is perhaps a little unfair in his condemnation of it. Inhibition and quiescence is, after all, preferable to the jubilation and acquiescence Hitler encountered among the German substitute for intelligentsia. The paranoid fear of the new regime may be gauged by the new censorship laws passed and the self-righteous pomposity of the language in which they were couched. An order of September 4, 1936 required the destruction of all books of "Socialist or Communist tendencies" as "a matter of public health." Another order, of December 24, 1936, decreed illegal "the production, sale and circulation of books, periodicals, pamphlets and all kinds of printed matter or illustrations of a pornographic nature, or of Socialist, Communist, *Libertarian or generally disruptive tendencies.*"[10] There is something about the wording of this that reminds one uncomfortably of the almost contemporary *autos-da-fé* in which the best part of German literature was thrown into the flames by "moral thugs and mental nullities." Under such conditions theater, of course, could not flourish. Socio-political conditions such as these call for an automatic revival of the well-made play in its blandest form. Theater becomes escape entertainment pure and simple. The hard edges of ideas are beveled off until the *pièce* becomes so *bien faite* that it can be rolled smoothly on to the stage with no danger of anyone's attention being aroused by the steady drone of its progress. Adolfo Torrado, the most successful playwright of the period, described one of his many indistinguishable plays as "a little recipe from my modest carpentry shop."[11] That summed up the period's playwriting perfectly, just as the intellectual climate of the time may be judged by Jacinto Benavente's lament in 1946 to the effect that the rabbits are taking over Australia, the Negroes those of the United States in which they are in the majority, and the yellow peril the world.[12] Nothing could more accurately and more sadly confirm Ortega y Gasset's poetically worded prediction of 1937 than this almost incredible remark by Benavente, who, twenty-four years earlier, had been Spain's second winner of the Nobel Prize for Literature awarded, in accordance with the wishes of the founder, to writers who advance the cause of humanity. Looking back on the wreckage of the Spanish intellect that Ortega had predicted, Luís Martín-Santos put it this way in his novel *Tiempo de silencio*, "The giants that were the windmills of long ago are the ghosts of our desires today."[13] Later on in this extraordinary novel, which serves as a poetic summing-up of post Civil War Spanish society, Martín-Santos sketches a mordant vision of Spain as a silent, quiescent, castrated nation: "We are dried mummies stretched out in the pure air of the meseta, hanging by a rusty wire, waiting for our small silent ecstasy."[14]

It would be unfair to say that Spain has not changed. The initial and natural feelings of insecurity of a government that has taken power by force against the most determined resistance of a large part of the populace, the enforced isolation of Spain during the Second World War, and the extreme economic debility that was inevitable after such a destructive conflict have all passed. The sentiments expressed by a Benavente in his senility or an Arias Salgado in his prime are held today only by a few die-hards. Quiescence has been replaced by hope; economic debility by comparative prosperity. Spain is no longer an isolated peninsula separated from Europe by the Pyrenees and from America by the sea. It has become as Europeanized as England and as Americanized as West Germany. Needless to say, neither of these conditions is utopian; and sad to say, both of them apply to conditions social and economic but not artistic. Spanish art, and especially Spanish theatrical art, still lies under the needless and anachronistic yoke of the censorship.

In a world as perverse in its actions and as fragmented in its beliefs as the one we live in, nothing happens straightforwardly, everything paradoxically. The paradox of Spain's recovery is that it is to be attributed not so much to hard work and good management as to poverty and de-Hispanization. Spain, which when it was a great nation, imposed itself on the world, has risen from the nadir of poverty and helplessness by subjugating itself to the world. The post

10

Civil War government was no shrewder than previous Spanish governments, and managed Spain no better. As Gerald Brenan has said, Spaniards "suffered from a disease which radiated from above downwards. And the chief symptom of that disease was the dissociation of the political system and [the men who] . . . operated it from the social and economic needs of the country."[15] This is as true as ever though in all fairness it should be noted that the disease is not peculiar to Spain: its symptoms have reached epidemic proportions in the United States since the onset of the Vietnam War, to go no further. Spain's poverty—that is, its government's inability to bring about its recovery from the Civil War by economic policy—is the direct cause of its present prosperity and de-Hispanization. A poor country has a low cost of living in comparison with richer countries. Devaluation of its currency makes the difference even greater. Hence the beginning around 1959 of the tourist trade, which was rapidly to become Spain's leading industry and its economic savior. But at the same time that it has set Spain on its feet economically, tourism has transformed it by inundating it with all that is most vulgar and undesirable in the rest of Europe and in America. For the first time in its history Spain is in danger of losing its uniqueness and individualism; and the economic prosperity for the sake of which it is doing so is largely illusory. For the majority of the populace the conditions of poverty still prevail, and for the intelligentsia the complete freedom which alone can enable them to produce the art and thought that is the life blood of a national culture remains suppressed.

Prosperity brings complacence. For Spain's *nouveaux riches* the criticism and reform that is implicit in the free exercise of art is anathema. Those who could support the theater are too busy accumulating money, consuming it conspicuously, and fearing its loss through reform or re-distribution. For the *parvenu* conservatism has always been the keynote of public behavior. No one fears a rocking boat more than one who has just stepped aboard with his newly acquired possessions still imperfectly balanced in his arms. Nothing illustrates this attitude better than two interviews with the new breed of Spanish businessman recorded by Chandler Brossard. The first is with a successful executive in his late thirties:

What if there is not political freedom? It that the most important thing in life, that ritualistic gesture of self-determination that is

11

everywhere just a ritual? The Spanish economy is rising and everybody is happy about it. . . . Somebody should tell those fools to stop causing trouble. It is a damn good thing what the government said—they will draft the protesting students if they keep up their nonsense. Fun is fun. But enough is enough. . . . Oh, there are some wrong things going on, but it is the same all over the world. . . . I can do business with anyone. That is my kind of freedom.[16]

The other interview, almost identical in the sentiments expressed, is with a man who lived many years abroad:

I discovered that one can really do whatever one wants here. You are rewarded for your effort. The business possibilities are unlimited. Each year our concern does better and better. We are doing business with firms all over the world now. The government does not interfere with us at all. I am not interested in politics, and that is the way it should be. These people who are are playing a very dangerous game with themselves. Why don't they just settle down to living their own lives? What is all this foolish noise? These demonstrations? Who are they doing any good? . . . I have a lovely new apartment and I have a wonderful girl. And I travel a good bit. What more should I ask of this world? Should I throw all this away for some crazy political ideology? . . . I do not intend to wreck myself with such foolishness. Things are very good now.[17]

Luís Martín-Santos gives us a powerful impressionistic picture of the results of this attitude:

. . . the ephemeral nocturnal city of closed churches and open taverns, flickering electric signs and speeding cars. Cars driven by raving madmen through the intersections of main streets. Convertibles with tops down in the cold evening air flaunting the blonde hair or the mink stoles of expensively dressed women. Silverplated expensive cars, closed, hiding the mask of drunken brutality. Enormous, powerful cars like elegant whales sliding along slowly with a lecherous roll. Cars launched like projectiles toward some tangible future pleasure.[18]

With this picture of sybaritic materialism and conspicuous consumption, where possession is an end in itself and effete comfort is raised to the status of an ideal, Martín-Santos shows the results of the businessman's attitude to the issues of life. In its essentials Spain has merged with the countries whose tourists are the source of its present prosperity. Like the United States and West Germany, by using what was probably the only possible way to raise itself out of the economic pit into which the Civil War had plunged it, Spain has immolated its essential characteristics on the altar of unthinking ease and unprincipled security. This tragic error and its effect on the Spanish mentality is one of the most important themes of the new Spanish drama.

If complacency and a yearning for stability at any price appear to be among the chief characteristics of Spain today, we must remember that they are confined to the visible part of the populace. The old land-owning families—the self-styled "*gente*" as opposed to the "*pueblo*"—which have managed to remain rich and prominent at the expense of others for centuries and the *nouveaux riches* who have known how to take advantage of the new tourist-stimulated prosperity are the immediately visible segments of Spanish society. Underneath, however, the picture is different. Part of the population is contentedly quiescent, satisfied to plod through their lives as if on a treadmill as long as they can remain confident that the machine is steady and moves at a comfortable and unchanging pace. The rest of the population seethes inwardly. Recognizing the uselessness of movement and wearied, in any case, of violence, they bide their time, hoping for a change in government. Meanwhile their views, whether expressed in art or in politics, remain suppressed by a government over-cautious to the point of paranoia. It would not be fair, however, to attribute the censorship entirely to paranoia or to a politically unrealistic conception that sees the Civil War as having saved Spain from a Communist Republic. Suppression of the opposition is a tradition in Spain. The short-lived Republic created when Alfonso XIII was ousted was Spain's first experience of democratic government. Like the Weimar Republic, it failed because the habits of millennia cannot be reversed overnight. Spain had always been a polarized society with an economic oligarchy, usually ruling indirectly, on one side and the exploited masses on the other. Except for the brief hiatus of the Republic it was to continue to be so.

The polarization of Spain—its development of a tradition of repressive dictatorship on the one hand and a will toward anarchic individualism on the other—may be traced to its isolation from the mainstream of European political thought as a result of its decline from world power in the seventeenth century. Drawing in upon itself, it became an enclave in which, politically and socially, time stood still and all outside influences were bitterly opposed. This self-imposed isolation had an extremely curious effect. The geographical differences within the peninsula became more pronounced as the need for unity against common foes and the pride engendered by successful nationalistic ventures disappeared. The separate peoples and cultures that constituted the Spanish nation tended to break off and to resent the Castillian efforts to propagate by force, if necessary, the myth of unity under the aegis of a Castile whose principal industry was bureaucratic administration. Thus Spain split up unofficially into sub-groups, each of which developed in its own way. Angel Ganivet developed an interesting theory of Spanish character in his *Idearium español* when he distinguished between insular, continental, and peninsular character, asserting that the last-named is obsessed with the idea of freedom and independence, while the first two are primarily concerned with aggression and defence, respectively.[19] This is, however, an over-simplification, as is Ganivet's assertion that the Spaniard is basically an anarchist because in all his wars he has fought essentially as a guerrilla.[20] Ganivet comes closer to the truth when he says that no nation has been more contemptuous of the administration of the law.[21] But it would hardly be accurate to use this statement as proof that the Spaniard is basically an anarchist. A society of anarchists produces no conflicts and no philosophical polarizations except individual ones. The strife that has been endemic in Spain during the last two centuries must be attributed to the mutual enmity of proliferating *groups*, not individuals. Spain, as one historian has put it, "shows perhaps the greatest degree of adjustment to subgroup conformity found in any large Western country."[22]

Prior to the decline of Spain as a world power it had, of course, always been governed by an absolutist system. With the decline of royal absolutism the schisms within Spanish society became more and more evident. Absolutism became something that had to be imposed rather than something accepted as a fact of existence. Hence the polarity of groups, the unwillingness to accept central authority, and the consequent total moral rectitude assumed by the group that we have come to recognize as characteristic of Spain. Such a situation could produce only a proliferation of separate states or a repressive dictatorship. And indeed, partially as a result of such deliberate isolationist moves as Floridablanca's *cordon sanitaire* in the 1790's, Spain became virtually a laboratory model of the techniques of dictatorship. The isolationism of Floridablanca separated Spain from Europe almost completely. The philosophical enlightenment in the rest of Europe was anathema to Floridablanca's ministry, and all original thought was looked on as government property to be regulated, censored, and, if dangerous, suppressed altogether.[23]

Liberal democracy has attracted only a small portion of the Spanish people over the years—and not even all of its intellectuals.[24] Instead Spain has experienced a succession of polarized situations subject to pendulum swings from one extreme to the other. The most obvious examples of this are the anarchists on the one hand and the Carlist *requetés* on the other. The anarchists, though impractically idealistic, can at least be admired for their theories, while their outbursts of violence against the establishment clerical and capitalistic, however pointless, deplorable, and futile, may be ascribed to a natural reaction of pent-up frustrations against a system that quite frankly considered them to be sub-human. Apart from the characteristically Spanish violence of the reaction, furthermore, there was little to distinguish the extreme radical parties of Spain from those of other European countries. It is at the other end of the political pendulum that Spain demonstrates its uniqueness. As Unamuno put it when considering the purely theoretical concept of an average Spaniard, "Unfortunately, there isn't any average Spaniard; in Spain we only have extremes."[25] The mentality represented by one of Ferdinand VII's propagandists who said "Where there is industry, liberty is easily born" is typical of this other end of the pendulum.[26] The statement is interesting for two reasons: the implicit assumption that liberty is undesirable and the unrealistic and anachronistic desire to maintain a feudal society of peasantry and all-powerful, paternalistic (though not necessarily in a benign sense) landowners. The attitude of the landowners that is implied is the one described by Blasco Ibáñez in one of his novels: "To Dupont every master held his position by divine right. God desired the existence of rich and poor, and those at the bottom should obey those at the top because it was ordained by a social hierarchy of celestial origin."[27] There is a curious similarity between this attitude and that shown by Franco's description of himself on all Spanish coins as "Caudillo by the grace of God." Such a bland and unconscious assumption of rectitude is nothing new among Spanish political leaders. Franco is clearly convinced that liberalism and democracy cannot last and that the world is inevitably approaching his position, a viewpoint that puts him in the peculiarly paradoxical position of being a pioneer of reaction.[28] The roots of this attitude probably lie in the Carlist movement, that paradigm of irrational political thought, whose members unthinkingly devote their lives to fighting for genealogical minutiae.

The first Carlist revolt was the Catalonian uprising of 1827,[29] an event that is still interesting to students of the Spanish character in its more curious aspects since it shows a streak that is conservative to the point of masochism. (Most of the Carlist fighters were peasants who were actually fighting for their own suppression.) The 1827 uprising was fought to abolish "novelties" like education and to restore the Inquisition. By a curiously symbolic coincidence the name of the reactionary Captain General of Catalonia was España. His "mindless absolutism" and "tyranny . . . converted Barcelona to liberalism."[30] Catalonia, the most cosmopolitan part of Spain, was never, in any case, a fertile breeding-ground for reaction; and Carlism subsequently found its strength in the isolated mountain fastnesses of Navarre.

In the latter part of the nineteenth century weird peculiarities of thought continued to appear, such as Ramón Nocedal's Integralist Party, a group that splintered off from Carlism and sought to bring about the kingship of Christ instead of Don Carlos.[31] The Marqués de Pidal, a politician of the 1880's, maintained that all modern thought was a "total error" beside "the unique total truth of Thomism."[32] As one reads about men like Nocedal, Pidal, and even Menéndez y Pelayo, who, at least, surrounded his medievalism with an aura of learning, one cannot help thinking of them as dinosauric throwbacks, strange monsters bellowing their prehistoric calls over the arid Castillian plains as if they were still steaming primeval marshes. It is no wonder that even enlightened intellectuals like Unamuno sometimes despair of the possibility of a free society and irritably deliver themselves of remarks like "El pueblo necesita un mesías—digamos un cacique—y lo busca; y si no lo halla, lo inventa. . . ."[33] There is an equally cynical element in Ganivet's remark that, in order to restore the spiritual essence of Spain it is necessary to replace the heart with a stone and to throw a million Spaniards to the wolves, if they are not all to be thrown to the swine.[34] The

16

despair of the Spanish intellectual has bred cynicism in the past, and this cynicism has in turn bred brutality. But where the intellectual's brutality is theoretical and born of frustration, the brutality of the politician has always been practical and instinctive.

To return once more after a long historical detour to the problem of contemporary Spanish underground theatre, we can see that censorship is inevitably one of the chief aspects of this practical and instinctive repression. In a dictatorship censorship is automatic, and Spain has always been a dictatorship (even during the Republic there were periods of press censorship). Manuel Fraga Iribarne, who, as former Minister of Tourism and Propaganda, was responsible for the censorship bureau, attempted to justify the institution by asserting that there can be no complete freedom of expression anyway since the communications media would be controlled by high finance, by interested pressure groups, or by prominent families or willful individuals, if they were not controlled by the State. The State, as he sees it, is the "tutor normal del bien común" and should act as a brake on the barbarities that would otherwise be spewed out by the press.[35] There is nothing original about this defence of Fraga's, sophistic though it obviously is: distrust of public opinion and unbridled expression is endemic among Spaniards. Gerald Brenan traces the attitude exemplified by Fraga back to Cánovas and his inspiration of conducting rigged elections for "the common good." Cánovas based his theories on a study of the Conde de Olivares' ministry in the 17th century. Like Olivares and his successors, Cánovas believed that "the affairs of the country must be conducted by a small select class of politicians, the most intelligent and the most eloquent, the best-educated, *who could be trusted to do what was necessary.*"[36] This system, of course, has always been eased administratively by the fact that separation of governmental powers has never existed in Spain. Judges have always simply been government employees who took their orders from above.[37] The consequence of all this is that those in power look upon themselves as paternalistic (severity being part of their duty when the children become recalcitrant), while those out of power tend to look upon their masters the way the ancient tribe around Lake Nemi looked on their priest-king. The paternalist attitude to censorship is summed up by Fraga:

Now, to be sure, freedom of expression involves duties and responsibilities. For this reason it may not be applied without controls to matters affecting the security of society; expressions that tend to incite to violence or that seek to change the government by illegal means, or that compromise the peaceful relationships between people; expressions that incite people to commit criminal acts; obscene expressions or those dangerous to the young and directed to them; expressions prejudicial to the proper and independent administration of justice; expressions that injure literary or artistic copyright; expressions defamatory to the reputation of other persons, whether in a natural or a legal sense; expressions that fail to fulfill legal obligations assumed as a result of professional or contractual relations, particularly those that tend to reveal secrets concerning certain aspects of public affairs and confidential information received in a professional or official capacity, and, finally, those that injure the guarantees necessary for the prevention of fraudulent acts.[38]

It is surely needless to point out the catch-all provisions contained in this insouciantly frank summing-up of the Spanish censorship system. Anything that is considered pragmatically undesirable at the moment falls under the provisions. On the other hand, the basic ultimate ineffectiveness of the censorship system is implicit here as well. The system has been left purposefully vague so that anything can be subsumed under it. The corollary is that anything—if sufficiently indirect—can escape the censor. The decision is left to the individual censor, and interpretation of the law is purely arbitrary and pragmatic. The fact is that literature *cannot* be suppressed. The attempt to do so is futile and self-defeating. The Spanish new wave or "underground" drama, whether it is publicly produced or not, negates the censorship *by its very existence*. As José Castillejo put it, "the golden age of Spanish literature proves that wit can thrive under oppression."[39] Censorship is born of paranoia.[40] It has proved ineffective and will continue to become more and more ineffective. While it is true, as one observer of contemporary Spain has said, that "Censorship . . . has manacled the first minds in the land; it has driven poets, authors and artists into exile or into silence . . .,"[41] it is equally true that Spanish artistic life is in the process of recovery. The innate strength of the Spanish character is re-asserting itself, as Angel Ganivet foresaw it would always do. The essence of the Spanish character, he said, is the stoicism of Seneca, which consists of a belief in one's own innate strength, a resistance to all pressures from outside, an insistence on being one's own man—"al menos se puede decir siempre de ti que eres un hombre."[42] The hope of Spanish literature was perhaps best summed up by Miguel de Unamuno when he compared the intransigence of Don Quixote to all that was best in the Spanish character:

What, then, is the new mission of Don Quixote in the world of today? To cry aloud, to cry aloud in the wilderness. But the wilderness hears, though men do not hear, and one day it will be transformed into a sounding forest, and this solitary voice that falls upon the wilderness like seed will yield a gigantic cedar, which with its hundred thousand tongues will sing an eternal hosanna to the Lord of life and death.[43]

NOTES

1. In 1970 two cases illustrative of this were the recall of the complete edition of José Ruibal's *Los mendigos y seis piezas de café-teatro* (published by Escelicer) and the censoring of Diego Salvador's *Los niños* on the night of the dress rehearsal (it was produced later with the required changes).

2. The play was *Guadaña al resucitado* in the March, 1970 issue of *Primer Acto*.

3. Fernando Díaz-Plaja, *The Spaniard and the Seven Deadly Sins*, translated by J. I. Palmer (New York: Scribner's, 1967), p. 22.

4. Marta del Campillo, "How Catholic is Spain?" *Michigan Quarterly Review*, VIII, iii (1969), p. 199.

5. José Cela, *The Hive*, translated by J. M. Cohen (London: Gollancz, 1953), p. 19.

6. *Ibid*.

7. José Ortega y Gasset, *Invertebrate Spain*, translated by Mildred Adams (New York: W. W. Norton, 1937), p. 39.

8. *Ibid.*, p. 41.

9. Salvador de Madariaga, *Spain* (New York: Praeger, 1958), p. 253.

10. Allison Peers, *Spain in Eclipse* (London: Methuen, 1945), p. 113. Italics mine.

11. José Monleón, "Treinta años de teatro de la derecha," *Triunfo*, No. 401 (February 7, 1970), p. 24.

12. José Monleón, "Treinta años de teatro de la derecha," *Triunfo*, No. 403 (February 21, 1970), p. 30.

13. Luís Martín-Santos, *Time of Silence*, translated by George Leeson (New York: Harcourt Brace & World, 1964), p. 6.

14. *Ibid.*, pp. 244–45.

15. Gerald Brenan, *The Spanish Labyrinth* (Cambridge: Cambridge University Press, 1962), pp. 10–11.

16. Chandler Brossard, *The Spanish Scene* (New York: Viking Press, 1968), pp. 36–37.

17. *Ibid.*, pp. 104–105.

18. Martín-Santos, *op. cit.*, p. 63.

19. Ganivet elaborates this idea at considerable length, cf. Angel Ganivet, *Idearium español* (Buenos Aires: Espasa-Calpe, 1945), pp. 32ff.

20. *Ibid.*

21. *Ibid.*, p. 59.

22. Stanley Payne, *Franco's Spain* (New York: Thomas Y. Crowell Co., 1967), p. 74.

23. Raymond Carr, *Spain, 1808–1939* (Oxford: Oxford University Press, 1966), p. 72. In 1791 the entire periodical press was suspended. In 1793 a journal of ideas was effectively killed by requiring submission of articles for review a whole year before publication—a technique very similar to that still in use.

24. Madariaga, *op. cit.*, p. 127.

25. Miguel de Unamuno, *Obras completas* (Madrid: Afrodiso Aguado, 1958), V, 64.

26. Carr, *op. cit.*, p. 149.

27. Vicente Blasco Ibañez, *La bodega*, translated by I. Goldberg (New York: E. P. Dutton, 1919), p. 26.

28. Benjamin Welles, *Spain: The Gentle Anarchy* (New York: Praeger, 1965), p. 13.

29. Carr, *op. cit.*, p. 150.

30. *Ibid.*

31. *Ibid.*, p. 353.

32. *Ibid.*, p. 354.

33. "The people need a Messiah—or let us say, a boss—and they look for him; and if they don't find him, they invent him. . . ." Unamuno, *op. cit.*, pp. 100–101.

34. Ganivet, *op. cit.*, p. 30.

35. Manuel Fraga Iribarne, *Horizonte español* (Madrid, 1966), p. 223.

36. Brenan, *op. cit.*, p. 4. Italics mine.

37. *Ibid.*, p. 8.

38. Fraga, *op. cit.*, p. 225.

39. José Castillejo, *Wars of Ideas in Spain* (London: John Murray, 1937), p. 73.

40. Madariaga attributes to Cavour the remark that "Any fool can govern with a press censorship" and points out that "Dictators rely on physical force and are, therefore, afraid of the moral forces that would be unchained by free criticism." (*Op. cit.*, pp. 346–47.)

41. Welles, *op. cit.*, p. 77

42. Ganivet, *op. cit.*, p. 9.

43. Miguel de Unamuno, *Essays and Soliloquies*, translated by J. E. Crawford Flitch (New York: Alfred A. Knopf, 1925), p. 124.

2

JOSÉ RUIBAL

José Ruibal was born near Pontevedra in Galicia in 1925. For the critic of modern Spanish drama there are two important implications in this bald statement. Ruibal belongs to a generation whose most formative years were spent during the Civil War, and he was born in Galicia. Galicia, the extreme northwest corner of Spain just north of Portugal, is separated from the rest of the country by natural barriers that make the landscape look more like Ireland than like the rest of Spain, where Galicians tend to be looked on with the same sort of suspicion that is accorded Irish tinkers in England. Galicians tend to be known for making cryptic indirect utterances, frequently in parable form. Unlike the direct and straightforward Castillian, the Galician prefers to talk around a subject and remain enigmatic and inscrutable. The Galician writer, then, usually clothes his meaning in fantasy and parable, and relies to a considerable extent on the rich folk literature available to him. Among the older generation of underground writers, Ruibal and José Maria Bellido, who is from the Basque country, tend to be cryptic, while Antonio Martínez Ballesteros and Juan Antonio Castro, Castillians both, tend to be much more direct.

José Ruibal came to writing late. In the 1940's he spent several years in Argentina and Uruguay, and it was there that he began to write and, gradually, to realize that his métier was the stage. Despite the fact that circumstances keep his work from being produced or published except in rare and unpredictable instances, Ruibal's writing is neither imitative nor untheatrical. First, he has traveled extensively (as has Bellido), and, second, he would have had a rich literary tradition to draw on even had he not traveled. Most of the underground dramatists, indeed, have not been outside Spain, and the books available to them inside Spain are severely limited. This limitation, it should be noted, is not simply a matter of the books being censored. Even when the books are available, they are frequently beyond the means of the dramatists, most of whom have been obliged to educate themselves as best they can. Self-education, no matter how haphazard, however, is usually better than education in a state-controlled system. A revealing aspect of the unavailability of books in Spain is the official equation of political trustworthiness and economic stability. As a result, some authors may be published in prohibitively expensive editions of their complete works while publication in cheap editions or of single works is forbidden. Since free lending libraries are virtually unknown in Spain, this policy effectively deprives Spain's underground intellectuals of many of the books that would interest them most.

The lack of cultural contact between Spain and the rest of Europe has not prevented all influence from penetrating to Spain's underground artists, however. Some authors have, like Ruibal, traveled and others are occasionally able to obtain foreign books and tell their fellow-writers about them. Nevertheless, although it has arrived at a destination very close to that of the rest of European drama, the Spanish underground drama has come there by a parallel route. The theme of the absurd, which has developed in Europe since the end of the Second World War as a result of the philosophical influence of Albert Camus, grew out of a perception of the incongruity between man and his environment, between the comforting and illusory structures of society and the reality of the instinctual brute forces of Nature. Spreading from the seminal drama of Beckett and Ionesco, with its philosophical roots in Camus and its theatrical roots in the theories that Antonin Artaud developed from his study of primitive psychology as expressed in drama and from the plays of Alfred Jarry, the absurdist drama has taken hold in the theaters of both Western and Eastern Europe.[1] The essence of the absurdist perception is a profound pessimism, a view of the human condition as hopeless, meaningless, and incomprehensible. Man is seen as being in the grip of a greater, impersonal, controlling power that annihilates him at will, removing him from an existence he never understood in which all the participants move aimlessly in mutually exclusive spheres running on courses unfathomable to their occupants. It is no criticism of the philosophical validity of this view to point out that this kind of teleological speculation is a perverse luxury: one thinks about the meaninglessness of the human condition when one has nothing better to do. Only in a society where the vicissitudes of the temporal condition have been smoothed out do the philosophically inclined have the leisure to contemplate the hopelessness and incomprehensibility of the cosmic condition. Absurdism is the modern equivalent of tragedy, which is no longer the pleasurably relieving Aristotelian contemplation of unconsciously self-willed individual misfortune, but the defeat of man at the hands of forces greater than himself, inimical to him, and incapable of being comprehended by him. Tragedy is possible as an art form only in a society that is basically free and affluent. In a society that is comparatively bare of other worries, men can afford time to worry about the cosmos. Vicarious indulgence in tragic feeling is an emotional luxury that only the inhabitants of a free society can wallow in. In a totalitarian society such indulgence is a hollow joke, a masochistic rubbing of salt into an open wound, rather than the satisfying release of emotional tension or the arousal of righteous indignation it ideally is. Furthermore, in a totalitarian society pessimism is discouraged since the whole point of such a society is redemption through faith in the state. Totalitarianism is religion reduced from the cosmic to the temporal level—which is why a sense of the tragic is also incompatible with religious faith. The so-called tragedies that have been written within a context of religious belief all boil down to a fall based on disobedience to the rules. The distinction between *Samson Agonistes* and socialist realism is stylistic, not philosophical—a matter of degree, not kind. In a totalitarian society we find surface literature, which is propagandistic when it is serious, quiescent and anaesthetic when it is not; and underground literature, which is critical and essentially hopeful. Men never seem to see the sun, for those who live in day find it obscured by blackest clouds, and those who live in night can only imagine its light and warmth.

In Spain the chief influence on the underground drama comes from within the Spanish literary tradition itself. The similarity to the avant-garde drama of the rest of Europe is purely formal, the leading themes of the plays being criticism, protest, and satire together with the optimism and constructiveness implicit in these. The formal similarity is, however, of the highest importance. While it has been pointed out before that the absurdist drama displays a pessimism deeper and different in kind from any that has gone before, it has not, I believe, been observed that its form also represents a complete break with tradition. Traditional drama had always consisted of an ordered sequence of events: a staged story. The meaning of the play had always been transmitted gradually through the accumulation of events and facts. In the absurdist drama the plots are frequently seemingly senseless or silly—because the plots per se (i.e., the logical realistic sequence of events) are unimportant. The absurdist drama is not a staged story: it is a staged symbol. The meaning of the play comes from a contemplation of the effect of the whole, rather than from a step-by-step progress. Atmosphere and suggestion are more important in this drama than narration. The same thing has occurred in Spain, though it has sprung from independent roots. The difference between the current generation of writers and writers like García Lorca, Salinas, Alberti, or Casona —the best of the writers whose careers were cut off or disrupted by the Civil War—is that the latter created essentially realistic plots with poetic language whereas the former base their works on an overall poetic symbol worked out in plain, straightforward language. Thus in contemporary Spanish drama an antipoetic language functions poetically. In the current underground drama, in other words, the language is realistic but the plot is not. The meaning of the play is contained in the sum total of its effect. While this technique is substantially the same as that employed by the absurdist dramatists of the rest of Europe, it is derived in the case of the Spanish drama from the work of Ramón del Valle-Inclán.

Ramón del Valle-Inclán is one of the most strangely neglected modern dramatists. Until the recent publication of Anthony Zahareas's massive collection of criticism no extended treatment of Valle-Inclán had appeared in English.[2] Spain has paid even less attention to her most important dramatist of the first half of the twentieth century. *Luces de Bohemia* (*Lights of Bohemia*, 1920),[3] his most seminal play, has yet to be performed in its entirety in Spain, and *Los Cuernos de Don Friolera* ("The Horns of Don Friolera," 1921) was given its first production there by the Madrid University Theatre as recently as 1968. This is all the more distressing because Valle-Inclán is, with Cervantes, the most acute of

24

all literary interpreters of the Spanish character. Despite the overt neglect to which he has been subjected, Valle-Inclán has been the acknowledged primary influence on the new wave Spanish dramatists, both because of his innovations in dramatic form and because of his interpretation of the plight of the Spanish character. In Spain the tension and conflict that give the necessary vitality to all drama have always sprung from the situation created by a simultaneous devout belief in the Church and an instinctive enmity to subjugation by the State (which in Spain has always to a considerable extent been coeval with the Church), caused by the exaggerated and often grotesque anarchic individualism so characteristic of the Spanish temperament. The paradox of this clash between an uncompromising insistence on the validity and primacy of the subjective vision and a simultaneous untroubled surrender to the narcosis of the Trinitarian incense is nowhere more neatly summed up than in that most seminal of all Spanish figures, Don Quixote. Valle-Inclán's contribution consists in perceiving the tension with which Cervantes imbued Spanish literature and "esperpentizing" it. The "esperpento" is an art form invented by Valle-Inclán. It is a way of viewing the world as a grotesque parody of itself, like seeing "reality" as reflected in a concave mirror. This method has, of course, obvious affinities with surrealism, as well as with the view of most contemporary dramatists (Dürrenmatt is the most outstanding example) that the essential tragedy of life can be endured only indirectly—through the medium of comedy. In this method of writing the artist must rise above his subjects, must assume the position of a malicious puppeteer. The author is no longer part of the conflict, describing it from within: he is commenting on it objectively, seeking a way to free his fellow men from the dilemma. The dramatic tension is no longer necessarily created by the conflict between individualism and religion, for in our world, whether in Spain or elsewhere, the conflict is as often between the individual and the state or between the individual and social tradition or psychological repressions.

Valle-Inclán himself described the method of the "esperpento" in these words:

. . . there are three ways of observing the world artistically and aesthetically; on one's knees, standing up, and raised in the air. When one looks at reality from one's knees—and this is the oldest position of literature—the characters, the heroes, are given a condition that is superior to the human condition . . . . There are created, in a manner of speaking, beings superior to human nature: gods, demigods and heroes. There is a second way, . . . and that is to look at the . . . protagonist[s] . . . as if they were our brothers, as if they were ourselves . . . And there is a third way, and it is to look at the world from a superior plane and to consider the characters of the plot as being inferior to the author . . . with a point of irony . . . . This is a manner which is very Spanish . . . And it is this . . . that moved me to change my literature and to write the "esperpentos," the literary genre that I baptize with the name, Esperpentos.[4]

The work of José Ruibal also adopts this style. As with Valle-Inclán and as with Dürrenmatt, the play becomes a cohesive unit in which the plot has meaning only as an entity, as a symbol of the meaning of the whole, and in which the author is "raised in the air" and controls the action from a superior plane. The principal difference between Valle-Inclán and Ruibal is that between the end of the former's career and the beginning of the latter's the Civil War was fought. No contemporary Spanish writer has been able to escape the burden of that event anymore than any responsible contemporary German writer has been able to escape the experience of the Second World War and the events that led to it.

Ruibal began writing while living in Argentina in the early 1950's. His first effort was a one-act farce called *La ciencia de birlibirloque* ("The Science of Blarney," 1956), based on a Galician folk tale. The following year he produced his first important effort, *Los mendigos* (*The Beggars*).[5] This represents a tremendous advance over Ruibal's first play. In one year he moved from naive farce to the form that has become characteristic of his later, mature work. *The Beggars* takes place in an imaginary country filled with maimed beggars and over-run by camera-bearing tourists in the guise of various animals who chatter about the "picturesqueness" of the beggars while disregarding their condition. That condition is determined by the triumvirate that rules the country, consisting of a dog (who is a general), an ass (who is Chief of Police), and a crow (who is a priest). All three of them are ineffectual, bumbling, brutal fools, however; and the real power in the country is in the hands of the Minister of Propaganda (portrayed as a parrot), who veers with every wind and sells his voice to the highest bidder but is asphyxiated by the truth at last. *The Beggars* shows the ultimate uselessness of repression, for as often as the beggars—the common people—are shot down, they rise again.

There are several themes and devices in *The Beggars* that are common to much of the underground drama. Some of these devices —for example, the universal habit of setting the plays in an imaginary country and frequently giving the characters distinctly non-Hispanic names—are clearly designed to lessen the chances of censorship. Censors, being *sui generis* creatures of sharply limited intelligence, can frequently be bamboozled by such comparatively simplistic subterfuges. The imaginary setting, however, is not used solely as a cunning assault on the censor's powers of perception; it is obviously an effective device for universalizing the play. It is also a necessary device, for to write plays that refer only to Spain's present situation would be puerile in the extreme; and the fact is that the plays of the underground all have themes that are applicable to the world today as a whole. *The Beggars*, for example, although it is unusual in having a specific reference to Spain in the introduction of the figure of Cervantes as part of the Chorus, is a play about any underdeveloped or subjugated country today. It could refer to almost any East European or South American country at least as well as to Spain. The extensive animal symbolism in *The Beggars*, while not peculiar to Ruibal, is characteristic of his work. As a satiric device animal symbolism is unsurpassable, for while it may frequently be excessively obvious, its visual quality makes it ideal for the instant comprehension necessary in stage production. Ruibal's use of this device is particularly effective as he is a master at suiting the physical and connotative qualities of the animal to the individuals or types he is satirizing. The incomprehension of the tourists who comprise the major industry of underdeveloped countries—that is, the major source of revenue and, therefore, the power of those whose interest it is to keep the country underdeveloped—is superbly shown through the use of giraffe figures peering amiably and enthusiastically down on what they see shortsightedly as "picturesque folk life" instead of as common human misery. The beggars, whom the tourists fail to see as reflections of themselves, but without money and the freedom it brings, function both as a choral group commenting on the action and as a symbol of defiance and indestructibility. In one form or another the beggars will be there when the dog, the ass, and the crow will be gone.

Ruibal's play is a celebration of the indomitable qualities of human beings in the face of adversity.

El bacalao (*The Codfish*, 1960) is a wildly comic satire on governmental red tape in which two minor bureaucrats who live, as one of them puts it, "in the very heart of our country . . . like the worm inside the apple," dream that they are administering justice in a land where the "law of the codfish"—dry and headless—reigns. Here the punishment for everything is beheading (one is reminded of Alfred Jarry's "disembraining machine" in the *Ubu* plays), which is seen as really merciful since "the head is the worst part of the body; ideas come out of it like putrid odors out of excrement." And once the head is off, the victim is ready to be received into the bosom of the sacred, all-embracing codfish. The sardonic joke here is that the fantastic dream-world of the two bureaucrats is precisely the same as their world in real life, enmeshed as they are in the labyrinthine folds of a hierarchical system in which they count only as ciphers. The image of the play is that of a world which has become an impersonal bureaucracy where the symbol (the codfish) has replaced life, and desiccation reigns supreme. The subject that Ruibal treats satirically here is treated realistically in several plays by Antonio Martínez Ballesteros, Carlos Muñiz, and Eduardo Quiles, in whose works bureaucratic lifelessness becomes a symbol of oppression in modern society.

El asno (*The Jackass*, 1962) [6] takes up the theme of colonialism and exploitation by American capitalism. From the viewpoint of the Spanish underground writers, a position they share with the majority of American liberals, the role of the United States as an apostle of democracy and as a bulwark against the spread of totalitarian Communism is no more than an elaborate theatrical posture masking an imperialism as cynical as the equally theatrical "white man's burden" concept of Victorian Britain. Whereas Britain carved out repressive political fiefdoms under the mask of a benign desire to spread the amenities of what was euphemistically designated as "culture and civilization," the United States is carving out economic fiefdoms under the guise of charitably spreading democracy and higher standards of living. This attitude towards the United States on the part of the underground authors is not so much inimical as it is disillusioned, and, like all their work, basically optimistic. They do not use Communism as a target for their satire since the elimination of totalitarianism in the satellite countries could be accomplished only by complete change rather than by the reform from within that remains a possibility in a democratic country—or even in a nominally democratic one.

The idea for *The Jackass* first came to Ruibal while he was living in Argentina and Uruguay in the early fifties, and the setting, though unspecified as usual, reflects those surroundings. An unmistakably American salesman named "Mr." sells to the most enterprising—and most crooked—of the peddlers in a small marketplace an electronic jackass that can do everything: it talks, makes stock market forecasts, cooks food, performs plastic surgery, and prints phony contracts, among other accomplishments. But while it enables its so-called owner (he is permanently in debt to the company that manufactures it) to enslave his fellows, it, in turn, enslaves him. The animal symbolism is here confined to the jackass, which is a commentary simultaneously on the country that manufactures it and on the "get-rich-quick-by-any-means" ideals it represents.[7]

Direct examinations of the mechanics of political totalitarianism are necessarily rare in the underground drama. Although both plays are allegorical in their approach and applicable to other countries quite as easily as to Spain, *Su majestad la sota* ("His Majesty the Jack," 1966) and *El hombre y la mosca* (*The Man and the Fly*, 1968)[8] both clearly are inspired directly by the situation in Spain today. *Su majestad la sota* is an allegorical depiction of the principal methods used by totalitarian rulers to maintain themselves in power. The two chief methods of doing this are open repression and anaesthesia of the populace to the point where they lose consciousness of self. Ruibal uses the kings from the deck of cards to illustrate these methods. The kings are in competition with each other for the hand of the princess of an imaginary country—the vexing question of the Spanish Succession is touched on here—and each describes his own system for ruling effectively. The King of Spades represents militarism (the suit is called "Swords" in Spanish) and wants to declare permanent martial law; Hearts suggests love, liberality, and permissiveness, so its king will rule by declaring the taverns national monuments; Clubs wants to preserve the status quo through repressive police measures; and Diamonds proposes to rule by financial corruption and wants to introduce a roulette table into every home. Immobility and repression, alcohol and gambling —the latter the two most effectual forms of social anaesthesia— are the classic methods whereby totalitarian governments remain in power and are allegorically portrayed in this play. However, none of these systems is good enough in itself. Nowadays a complex, cynical, and opportunistic pragmatism is necessary, so the figure of *la sota*—the knave or Jack—who combines all the qualities of all the kings, and who has been ruling the country all along, continues to rule.

The Man and the Fly is undoubtedly Ruibal's masterpiece and one of the most important plays of our time. As a piece of political analysis stated in artistic terms it is unequalled, and, quite independently of any direct influence, it displays some of the principal themes and techniques of the modern European theater. Indeed, it combines the best of two worlds, for Ruibal shows a definite connection with the tradition of Spanish literature and its most characteristic themes in this play as well. There had already been signs of this in a rather overt way (by which I mean that it was superimposed on the tradition rather than integrated with it) in the introduction of Cervantes into *The Beggars*, where Ruibal used the technique of simultaneous time which had been worked out by Thornton Wilder in *The Skin of Our Teeth* and *Our Town* and carried on by Max Frisch in *The Chinese Wall*. In *The Man and the Fly* the use of traditional elements from Spanish literature is far more subtle and effective. These elements are three in number: the atmosphere of dream-fantasy that pervades the play, the introduction of the supernatural—and the consequent elevation of the action to a higher plane and into a different perspective—and the setting of the action in an apparent unreality which is in fact a higher reality, a reality stripped of everyday accoutrements to show its quintessence. The first two of these elements hardly require elaboration for those familiar with the tradition of Spanish literature, but the last is somewhat more complicated since it demonstrates Ruibal's empathy with current trends in the drama of other nations as well. What is so interesting about this empathy is that it may very well be unconscious—a spontaneous and independent perception of the same philosophical viewpoint, since most of the literature in which it is contained is unavailable in Spain.

The Man and the Fly takes place in that unnamed, mythical, and symbolically representative country that is so ubiquitous in the new Spanish drama. The country has been ruled for seventy "peaceful" years by El Hombre, who is creating a double in his magnificent crystal dome to carry on his work after his death and give birth to the myth of his immortality. In this country people sleepwalk through their customary routines, much as they do in the so-called "realistic" plays of the journeyman plodders who supply the staple fare of New York's Broadway, London's West End, or Paris's boulevards. But the "real" reality, the reality they dare not even think about, is the barren plain devoid of flora and fauna, like the barren heath in *Waiting for Godot*, in which they live, and against which they have desperately thrown up psychological barriers (self-delusions, drink, social conventions, routines) and material bulwarks (technological protection, television, movies, sports). Also real, of course, is El Hombre and his magical, dazzling crystal dome. Ruibal thus shows us the quintessential reality behind the façade of life in this play.

Just as the central symbol of the play, the crystal dome, is an architectural construct, so is the play. Reading this play one perceives a carefully planned structure of interlocking themes that gives an overall effect of architectural cohesion and consistency. In the depiction of El Hombre and El Doble and their perverse relationship one sees a steady progression similar to that found in the structure of the ancient Greek drama. There is the sense of ineluctable fate in the realization that El Hombre cannot last and in the audience's sardonic knowledge of the vanity of his attempt to immortalize himself by reproducing himself; there is the sense of inexorable time in El Hombre's impatient efforts to complete his task of animating his puppet; and there is the sense of the culmination of destiny as we see the inevitable collapse of all these grandiose plans at the end as El Hombre's human robot falls apart, and, like Peer Gynt, whose soul Ibsen symbolized by an onion, reveals himself as all husk and no core. It is surely no accident that Ruibal has used the fly as his symbol of retribution, just as Jean-Paul Sartre did in his modernization of the Aeschylean Furies of the *Eumenides*.

The symbols are the cement in the architectural structure of this play. Besides the fly that finally destroys the old order, we have the superbly conceived double symbol of the crystal dome. The dome is the place in which El Hombre has immured himself for the last seventy years and from which he rules his arid and sterile domain. As a reminder of the crystal spheres which bound and enclose the universe in Ptolemaic astronomy, it symbolizes the archaic system under which El Hombre lives and rules. But it is also a huge and elaborate structure whose foundations, we are told, are the bones of El Hombre's enemies; and it is planned by El Hombre as his own tomb, where, by a self-willed act, he will immolate himself and become immortal through his surrogate. As such it reminds one irresistibly of the marble, granite, and porphyry tomb into which the Chief of Police descends in Genet's *The Balcony*, there to sit and wait for two thousand years until he becomes part of the matrix of universal human mythology.

El Hombre understands that he has been in power for only seventy years, a totally insignificant period in the context of human history, and that he would be forgotten as soon as he is gone. So he has decided to perpetuate himself symbolically through the device of creating his own *doppelgänger*, a double who will continue his work and, presumably, will create other doubles on to infinity, until the image of El Hombre is indelibly imprinted on the collective human consciousness. The seventy-year peace of which El Hombre is so proud is also symbolic, for it is, as a well-known American hymn has it, a "peace that passeth understanding"—a "peace" of utter sterility and quiescence. The land outside the crystal dome is like the darkness outside Ptolemy's crystal spheres: no life, no vegetation, and, of course, no faith. Faith, of a spurious kind, is simulated inside the dome, whose walls are painted to resemble stained glass windows and are decorated with trophies of the hunt, fishing, and of war—lifelessness and sterility inside and out. Inside the dome, also, as in Genet's Balcony—the "House of Illusions," as Genet calls it—everything is false. The grotesque and monstrous El Hombre does nothing but dream his vainglorious dreams, letting papers and dust pile up, making his double jump around like a bird in a cage, and teaching him vicious morsels of "realpolitik" like "the lie is the only truth that can be permitted in a constructive political system." There is one other unconscious literary parallel in Ruibal's work, and that is to Erich Kästner's wonderful play *Die Schule der Diktatoren* ("The School for Dictators"). In this play the dictator has died, but no one knows it, except a *junta* of generals who really govern the country and keep a supply of a dozen or more doubles on hand, constantly training more. Whenever one of the doubles playing the dictator shows a sign of independence, he is killed off and replaced by another one from the school.

I have spoken so far about Ruibal's excellent command of the devices of allegory and of fantasy and of his place in the mainstream of current avant garde literature. I should like to say a few words, in conclusion, about his style and his use of imagery, in both of which he seems to me to be outstanding. Style and imagery as satiric instruments both reach a high point of development in this play. The passage in which El Hombre refers to bullets as doves' eggs incubated in machine-gun nests seems to me one of the most trenchant of modern poetic images; and the lyric passage immediately following it in which El Hombre pirouettes around the dome chirping about the dove of peace perched on torpedoes, pistols, tanks, hand grenades, and atom bombs is stage satire carried to its highest possible level.

The parallel between El Hombre and El Doble and some of the world's more recent political events is obvious. The play is a superb take-off (unintended, though prophetic, since it was written earlier) on the Johnson-Humphrey relationship as well as on the DeGaulle-Pompidou succession, to mention only two.

The Man and the Fly is the high point of Ruibal's dramatic production so far, although his work continues to be innovative and consistently interesting. In 1969 he published *Los mendigos y seis piezas de café-teatro*, which includes six skits written for cabaret theater. Before the edition could be put on sale, however, the censors decided that the dissemination of the title play might contribute to the fall of the government and banned the book. It was thereupon re-issued as *El mono piadoso y seis piezas de café-teatro* ("The Pious Monkey and Six Pieces of Café Theatre").[9] *El mono piadoso* is actually a libretto for a form Ruibal calls "pocket opera." It was first produced in 1970 with music by Pedro Luis Domingo and is a burlesque attack on American racism. It is set in the Central Park Zoo and involves one of the monkeys, who has discovered that he has a soul. At first a Southern racist wants to lynch him, but he is saved when a chorus of F.B.I. men points out that he is always fit to serve in the army and marches him off to fight for racism. Other café theater skits included in the volume are *Los ojos* ("The Eyes," 1968) and *El padre* ("The Father," 1968), plays in which Ruibal is concerned with the upbringing of children and the pressures on them to conform. Both plays end in a manner reminiscent of the antiparental violence of the German expressionist plays. *Los mutantes* ("The Mutants," 1968) and *El super-gerente* ("The Manager-in-Chief," 1969) both depict the mechanization of life and the dehumanizing effects of modern society.

The theme that Ruibal touched on briefly in the two last mentioned skits he developed fully in the ambitious and elaborately structured *La máquina de pedir* ("The Begging Machine," 1969).[10] This play was commissioned by the state-sponsored Teatro Maria Guerrero, but when it was finished it proved too difficult for the director of the theater and so far it has yet to be produced, though it has been translated into German. Up to a point the puzzlement of the director of the Maria Guerrero was understandable. *La máquina de pedir* is certainly one of the most complex plays of the modern stage, enormously difficult to produce, and by no means clear in its meaning on a first reading. It is, however, a play that would be far easier to understand were it staged properly since it is written in essentially theatrical terms. The mysteries of the text are caused by the difficulty of describing the effect of theatrical symbols in cold print.

The setting of the play is a fantastically luxurious apartment overlooking a beach. The stage is flanked by two enormous television sets which are really miniature stages in themselves and serve as entrances and exits for characters. In the middle of the stage there is a huge water tank with a yellow octopus inside it. A pipeline extends from the octopus to the sea, and every so often the octopus takes a deep breath, lets it out, and, lo and behold, a tiny oil tanker emerges from him and slides along the pipeline to the sea, growing as it goes. When it is not giving birth to oil tankers the octopus floats around in its tank signing checks and making business deals. The protagonist of the play is actually the octopus's recent bride, an extremely beautiful woman who has married the grotesque and much older octopus for his money in order to be able to use it for charitable purposes. Everyone she knows (as well as the general public, which avidly follows all her actions in the press) despises and envies her for marrying the octopus, but she does not care since it is all justified in her eyes by her hatred of poverty, which she now proposes to eliminate with the octopus's money. She has already distributed so much money through charitable organizations that poverty no longer exists in her own country. One of the television sets lights up and shows the current condition of the poor. They are now flush with money, food, drink, clothes, and jewels. But they are not happy. Poverty has been ingrained into them through generations and generations, and their sudden change in fortune gives them a feeling of uselessness. They die in droves—

some of overeating and indigestion, some of anxiety, others of too-sudden joy. They curse the Lady and want to kill her for having turned their lives upside down. On the other "screen" the rich are seen complaining of the sudden disappearance of the poor and the resultant lack of social equilibrium. Since they can no longer practice charity, their consciences keep bothering them. Some of them hoard poor people, keeping them locked up in safes, but the poor die anyway, crushed by their good fortune. Charity no longer exists and consequently the rich stream down to hell, creating a serious *lebensraum* problem down there. The rich, of course, also want to kill the Lady for upsetting their lives. In fact the whole country is in such an uproar over this disruption of the normal dog-eat-dog economic state that the Supreme Governing Council meets to discuss the crisis caused by the elimination of poverty. The Council consists of men who have computers and other electronic machinery instead of heads. Despite this, they are unable to find any solution other than the usual economic remedies of increasing the supply of money and the amount of expenditures. Finally a solution is produced by a Neapolitan parrot that picks the answer out of a pile with its beak: build a begging machine to perform the function of the poor and thus give the rich the illusion of virtue. The machine is built and marketed, becoming an enormous success—particularly in Asia and Africa, where poverty has always been a way of life. The poor are, of course, unable to compete with an electronic gadget that makes giving painless, since it does not make the rich uncomfortable by showing them the misery they are largely responsible for creating, and at the same time enables them to salve their consciences by giving away some of their surplus money. As a result, the poor die. The world thus becomes an earthly paradise where all social inequalities have been eliminated. However, the rich soon become tired of a world without social inequalities, but they are unable to do anything about it since, once they have submitted themselves to the machine, they have become irrevocably enslaved by it. Another economic problem now arises: since everyone has a begging machine, they no longer buy. This problem is solved by the creation of a new model, which not only begs but steals as well.

Long, rambling, frequently inchoate, *La máquina de pedir* has so many philosophical ramifications that it is almost impossible to enumerate all of them. The two principal objects of the author's satire are the hypocrisy of charity and the mechanization of life.

Ruibal portrays charity as an easy tranquilizer of the consciences of the rich, for whom the eternal division between their economic state and that of the rest of the world is an indispensable condition of existence. Just as good cannot exist without evil, as generations of theologians have never tired of informing us in their eager apologia, so the rich cannot exist without the necessary (to them) contrast of the poor. The analogy does not hold, as Ruibal shows us in his play, however, for while good and evil are necessary opposites, rich and poor are artificial differences.

Ruibal depicts the mechanization of life with his brilliant device of showing the ruling powers of the world as hybrid machine-men, their heads in the form of miniature computers if they are civilians and in the form of weapons if they are military. An American is irresistibly reminded of the uniformed robots in the Pentagon and the businessmen in the Cabinet, chosen less for their human qualities than for their success as calculating machines. Ruibal also continues his mastery of animal symbolism here. The yellow octopus who gives birth to oil tankers is the robber-baron businessman who cuts through all rules, operating unscrupulously in the single-minded pursuit of money. His success makes him an object of awe and respect to those whom he is swindling by manipulating the rules that they themselves have set to control his ilk. Like the bankers in Dürrenmatt's *Frank V*, the octopus is an atavistic animal who will inevitably be replaced by the dehumanized electronic man.

It is hard to predict at this point in what direction Ruibal will go. He has the talent and the versatility to accomplish almost anything in the theater, and the maturity and insight to treat any subject. The only conceivable obstacle in his path is the discouragement that might develop as a result of his inability to have his plays produced in his own country.

NOTES

1. For a full explanation of this development see the pertinent chapters in my *The Theatre of Protest and Paradox* (New York: New York University Press, 1971).

2. Cf. Anthony N. Zahareas, editor in chief, *Ramón del Valle-Inclán: An Appraisal of His Life and Works* (New York: Las Americas Press, 1968).

3. Translated by Anthony N. Zahareas and Gerald Gillespie in *Modern International Drama*, II, ii (1969).

4. Quoted in Anthony N. Zahareas and Gerald Gillespie, "Ramón María del Valle-Inclán: The Theatre of Esperpentos," *Drama Survey*, VI (1967), 9-10.

5. Translated by John Pearson in *Drama and Theatre*, VII, i (1968).

6. Translated by Thomas Seward in *Modern International Drama*, II, i (1968) and in George E. Wellwarth, ed., *The New Wave Spanish Drama* (New York: New York University Press, 1970).

7. The text of this play has also been adapted by the author into an opera libretto under the title *El asno electrónico* ("The Electronic Jackass," 1968).

8. Translated by Jean Zelonis in George E. Wellwarth, ed., *The New Wave Spanish Drama* (New York: New York University Press, 1970). The world premiere of the play was given at the State University of New York, Binghamton in November, 1971.

9. This curious situation was caused by the recent substitution of post-censorship for pre-censorship, i.e., previously manuscripts had to be submitted to the censors prior to publication; now anything could be published, but it was subject to scrutiny by the censors after publication and might therefore be recalled. Ostensibly a liberalizing move, it actually had the effect of making publishers and producers more cautious since the banning of a book after it had been printed or the prohibition of a play after it had been put into rehearsal involved far greater financial loss to the sponsors than the previous system. In the present case the recall of the original edition has resulted in a bibliographer's nightmare. The original edition was published as No. 632 of Escelicer's *Collección Teatro*. When *El mono piadoso* had to be substituted, the banned edition was treated as if it had never existed, and the new edition was given the same number in the series and the same copyright number. To save money, however, the six pieces of café theatre were not re-set, leaving a tell-tale gap in the pagination since *El mono piadoso* is three pages shorter than *Los mendigos*. Another curious aspect of the affair was that one of the *café-teatro* skits, *El rabo* (*Tails*) (translated by Marcia C. Wellwarth in *TDR*, *xiii*, iv [1969], pp. 157–59), which has had a great deal of trouble in getting licensed for performance because of its allegorical representation of political repression, was permitted to be printed.

10. *Die Bitte Maschine* (Basle: Kurt Reiss Verlag, 1970) and *La máquina de pedir; El asno; La ciencia de birlibirloque*, intro. by George E. Wellwarth (Madrid: Siglo XXI, 1970).

3

ANTONIO MARTÍNEZ BALLESTEROS

Antonio Martínez Ballesteros was born in Toledo in 1929 and still lives there. Growing up in the shadow of the Civil War and its aftermath, he had no opportunity to leave home or to obtain an education. Toledo is one of the most picturesque towns in Spain and is a haven for the German and American tourists who comprise its chief industry. For its natives it is, however, a symbol of provincial dullness where the social event of the day, the week, and the year is the *paseo*. A less likely breeding ground for dramatic genius could hardly be imagined. Not only is there no theater in Toledo, but the proximity of Madrid is of no help. For the average citizen of Toledo, particularly during the years in which Ballesteros was growing up, even the short trip to Madrid to see a theatrical production was prohibitively expensive. Nor, for that matter, was there anything worth seeing in the Madrid of those years. Ballesteros's decision to become a dramatist is, thus, all the more remarkable and can be explained only by an instinctive talent for the theater, the nature and extent of which the author himself can hardly have been aware of. That talent has been shown not only in the plays he has written, but also in the organization of an amateur theater in Toledo, where, as director, he has displayed an ability that outranks all but the foremost professional directors in Spain.

Ballesteros presents a stark contrast to Ruibal. Where Ruibal specializes in fantasy and parable, Ballesteros writes straightforward stories. The hard, uncompromising idealism of the Castillian replaces the indirect symbolism of the Galician. The struggle of Ballesteros to create drama in a stifling provincial environment, without the opportunity to learn about the theater by seeing it performed, is clearly reflected in the steady and remarkable progression of his art. Ballesteros's early plays are, as might be expected, more like dramatized essays, and are almost geometrically symmetrical in form.[1] Despite this, the innate theatricality of his talent is already evident in them.

Orestiada 39 (1960) is a retelling of the *Oresteia* in terms of the Spanish Civil War. One of the leading themes of the new Spanish drama is the necessity for reconciliation. Recognizing that to forgive and forget is totally alien to the Spanish character, the new Spanish playwrights have seen that it is hopelessly self-destructive to keep fighting the old battle, nursing grudges and bitterness that have been passed down from father to son. Regrets have become vain, and the only possible solution is to build anew. While the new thinkers of Spain may regret the particular state of affairs that has prevailed, they are pragmatic relativists who realize that the past cannot be undone, and the only sensible approach is the creation of improvements based on present conditions. *Orestiada 39*, like Bellido's *Football*, is an enlightened attempt in this direction, entirely free of the sedulous self-justification that characterizes an "establishment" play like Calvo Sotelo's *La muralla*.

Ballesteros sets his play in the period immediately following the Civil War. The Atreian household becomes a Nationalist colonel, his wife, daughter, and son, who has been wounded. Aegistheus is Eugenio Navarro, who started out in the Loyalist army (or "red army" in the cant of the Nationalists) and was later wounded after joining the Nationalists. On sick leave, he has been hanging around the house while managing the family's business affairs. Isabel-Electra tells her mother to get rid of Navarro or she will betray their relationship to her father. The story runs parallel to Eugene O'Neill's *Mourning Becomes Electra* until the killing of Christina-Clytemnestra and her lover. Then Alberto-Orestes has a vision of the Furies pursuing him and being called off by the Pacifier, who appears and announces that the consequences of the acts must be faced and the acts expiated before the land can be cleansed of the atmosphere of violence that motivated them.

While the plot of the play is reminiscent of the O'Neill trilogy, the ending is patterned on the classical model. There is none of O'Neill's interest in psychological forces as determinants of the characters' actions, since the play is a direct political allegory. The "pacifier" device may seem overly didactic, but it is no more so than the appearance of Athena at the end of the Aeschylean trilogy. *Orestiada 39*, like its Greek predecessor, is a plea for the replacement of self-seeking anarchy by law, of fragmentation by community. There is this difference, though. In the Greek play the advent of the *deus ex machina* was intended seriously and may be presumed to have been accepted in that spirit: the audience believed in Athena, and her speech confirmed the validity of the social system under which they lived. In Ballesteros's play, as in Bellido's *Football*, where a "great referee" is expected to descend from the sky and put everything right, the *deus ex machina* is a piece of wishful thinking. The reconciliation of which the Pacifier speaks has not come, nor does it seem likely to: Bellido's referee, of course, never comes to rectify the score of the game.[2]

Orestiada 39 was largely an experiment in the use of allegory through classical models. In *Los mendigos* ("The Beggars," 1961; not to be confused with José Ruibal's play of the same name)[3] Ballesteros creates his own symbols. *Los mendigos* is based on the central image running through most of Ballesteros's work: the modern state as bureaucracy. In Ballesteros's plays life is a pyramidal pecking order composed of hide-bound, frightened officials who have become dehumanized by the corruption of power and the worship of security. The result is a masochistic wallowing in unctuous servility combined with a sadistic display of brutish callousness to those below as compensation. The bureaucratic image gains additional strength in Ballesteros because it is also observed with a sardonic realism based on the author's own life and career as a civil service official. The hero in Ballesteros's plays is always the man on the lowest level of the pyramid who refuses to play the game—the persecuted outsider who reflects the author's own inviolable integrity and embodies his essential optimism and uncompromising honesty.

Los mendigos, written in 1961, does not have the maturity of Ballesteros's later plays. At the time, Ballesteros was still completely unknown and, though conscious of his talent, could see no way out of his hopeless situation. In no sense, however, is this or any of his plays strictly autobiographical, because the genius of

Ballesteros lies in his ability to use his own situation as a symbol of the plight of his country. The "beggars" of the play are all those who are trapped by economic pressure at their desks in the Great Office of the World, and are revenging themselves for the loss of their dignity and self-respect by barring those below them from access to what they themselves have lost. Those above are as trapped and pitiful as those below, for, as Ballesteros puts it, "nowadays there are beggars with cars and television." At the end the protagonist, who has lost his job by protesting on a matter of principle, begs for it back and so becomes one of the rest. In this early play Ballesteros has arrived independently at Brecht's axiom, "Erst kommt das Fressen, dann kommt die Moral."

Los mendigos was also the first play in which Ballesteros's other principle themes appeared. Like Arthur Miller, Ballesteros believes that the common man has sufficient dignity to bear the weight of tragedy, and that social position is no guarantee of innate nobility. Like Miller, too, he has the artistic capacity to transform the common individual into a representative figure embodying traits that the spectator can recognize in himself. This subjective psychological sensitivity is combined with an objective didacticism that takes the form of a powerful moral indignation aimed at repression, corruption, and human exploitation, and which Ballesteros presents in the form of a rational man attempting to survive in an insane world.

The plight of the rational man in an insane world now becomes the central theme of Ballesteros's work. The rational man is the man of good will, the instinctive humanist who believes that right must triumph, and who cannot believe that the world is merely a sardonic practical joke which may not even be intentional. Here Ballesteros differs from more worldly and pessimistic authors who see the issue of humanism as dead in a world that has rushed headlong beyond the point of no return into a state of atavistic irrationality.[4] The insane world in Ballesteros's plays takes the form of a self-worshipping bureaucracy—an all-encompassing machine that is mystically greater than the sum of the parts that compose it.

In *El pensamiento circular* ("Thought by Memorandum," 1963) Ballesteros meticulously develops his image of the world as a giant bureaucratic pecking order. The hero, as always in his plays, is the repressed, independent, and decent man who is trying to maintain his family on a minimal salary. He maintains his integrity by not becoming part of the servile order that is perpetuated by awarding substantial bonuses to boot-lickers in a seemingly endless hierarchy. The Director, who is the *bête noire* of the piece, is himself only a victim-cog in the machine, cringing to *his* superiors. The play is clearly a forerunner of *La colocación*, but it has moments of artistic maturity. For example, during the presentation of bonuses to the boot-lickers, the Director's speech is drowned out by the music and loudspeaker of a passing advertising procession and only isolated phrases, dealing with devotion to God, Country, and Work, are audible. There is fine dramatic irony here: the empty phrases of false devotion are drowned out by the raucous mendacity that is really the object of worship. The effect that Ballesteros produces with this scene is a coherent and immediately meaningful image. In art the closest approximation to this technique is the collage or the dynamic painting.

El pensamiento circular represents an advance over *Los mendigos*, both in technique and in philosophy. Both plays end in the defeat of the protagonist, but in the later play despair is replaced by a determination not to give in. Where in the earlier play the protagonist had to admit defeat at the end and became swallowed up in the grindstones of the machine, here he affirms his faith in the future. In his uncompromising determination and his will to persist he is the perfect exemplification of the "hombre duro"—the rational man in an insane world—so typical of Castillian life and literature.

The best play that Ballesteros has written on the theme of the "hombre duro" is *En el país de jauja* (*The Best of All Possible Worlds*, 1962).[5] In this play Ballesteros abandoned the office metaphor for the device of fantastic allegory. No longer dramatizing on the basis of his own experience, Ballesteros here creates his own dramatic world. In the plays based on the office metaphor, excellent though they are, there is nevertheless continually a feeling that they refer to specific things. They are not easy to lift out of their immediate context into one beyond office life. In *The Best of All Possible Worlds*, however, Ballesteros has adopted the device of fantastic allegory, favored by most of the new Spanish playwrights. This was done quite independently, to be sure, since at the time of writing Ballesteros was totally unaware of the existence of any other playwrights with even vaguely similar ideas.

The rational man in *The Best of All Possible Worlds* is Juan Pobre (John Poor), who is living in a state of semistarvation in a brutally repressive dictatorship. He sees a revolutionary being beaten up by the police and advises the Chief of Police, an old schoolmate, to feed him instead of beating him. The Minister of Repression also hears this advice, is deeply impressed, and offers Juan a job, which he declines to take. Juan's integrity finally lands him a twelve year jail sentence since an insane society cannot tolerate the presence of a single honest man. However, the most original aspect of the play is its treatment of the revolutionary. After Juan's advice about feeding him is followed, the revolutionary becomes a docile minion of the regime, endlessly stuffing himself with food and growing fat. Without ever having had the opportunity to know Brecht's works, Ballesteros here takes his thought one step further. Brecht said "Erst kommt das Fressen, dann kommt die Moral"—"First you fill your belly, then you think of right and wrong." However, Ballesteros perceived that once his belly is full, man no longer cares to think about right and wrong. Brecht's simplistic and humane solution turns out to be insufficient: only the downtrodden think of right and wrong and are, for the most part, quite willing to abandon the quest for the sake of comfort and security.

Ballesteros's treatment of the revolutionary leads him into another one of his principal themes: the instability of idealism in the face of the corrupting power of status and money. In *Las gafas negras del Señor Blanco* ("Mr. White's Sunglasses," 1966) Ballesteros again shows a finer perception of human psychology than Brecht's. He demonstrates once more that the proverb should read "Erst kommt das Fressen, dann geht die Moral"—"First you fill your belly, then right and wrong no longer matter." In this play the protagonist is a poor man who becomes rich and corrupted. He apes the manners of the moneyed class he has joined and feels that whatever he does is morally justified because he now has money, however dubiously he may have come by it. Ballesteros has written what is essentially a modern version of the medieval morality on the "Everyman" theme with the protagonist corrupted by Riches and Bad Deeds. In our time there is no longer any salvation, however: the protagonist has absorbed and accepted the morality under which he has grown up and re-applies it to perpetuate a vicious circle. Ballesteros's vision here, while not hopeless, is certainly cynical in the extreme. At the same time it should be noted that although this play is clearly inspired by the Spanish situation, it is in no sense a regional play. As in all of his plays—indeed, as in all of the Spanish underground drama—Ballesteros demonstrates the natural artist's innate and instinctive universalizing vision. The problems and situations he dramatizes are not peculiar to Spain, they are peculiar to all self-seeking societies; that is to say, to all post-tribal societies.

Precisely the same theme, though in a more direct and Brechtian style, is treated in *El camaleón* ("The Chameleon," 1967). The play begins with a panoramic and episodic view of a revolution and a bitter, satiric picture of the brutish essence of the military mind. Against this background, Ballesteros tells the story of Juan Lanas. Lanas is sentenced to death for killing his wife's lover in self-defense. Since the lover was a government official, killing him is interpreted as a political crime. Lanas escapes from prison in his cell-mate's coffin and goes abroad. In his adopted country he becomes John Lane, now a pro-government man. He climbs ruthlessly over his fellow workers and takes over the factory in which he worked when he first arrived. This makes him a widely honored public benefactor in the eyes of society, although he is, of course, thoroughly dishonest. Again Ballesteros's theme is the instability of personal honesty when faced with the temptations of affluence and security. Only the rational man who knows himself and has confidence in his own integrity—the "hombre duro"—can resist.

Though Ballesteros is quite capable of writing light comedies, there is always a mordant touch, typical of the comedies of a writer like Dürrenmatt. *Farsa de marionetas* ("Puppets' Farce," 1964) is an amusing satire on hypocritical sexual morality involving a man married to an excessively strait-laced woman who finds her double in a prostitute. The wife persuades the prostitute to work the classic bed-switch trick on the husband. While the wife is fooling her husband in this manner, the prostitute, carrying the wife's identity card, is killed in a traffic accident. Rejected by all her friends and unable to convince anyone that she really is the wife (the husband having meanwhile died of a heart attack), she has to become the prostitute despite all her strait-laced instincts. Ballesteros here shows us the reverse of the Brechtian process. The wife has everything at the beginning and has no thought of morality except in the purely conventional and formalistic sense of Puritanical sex repression; at the end the sudden loss of her money and social position forces her to give up her spurious principles and do whatever is necessary to survive.

44

Although the serious satiric intent of *Farsa de marionetas* is clear and trenchant enough, the overall atmosphere of the play is essentially farcical, and the humor cleverly based on the numerous mistaken identity situations. The same theme of social hypocrisy is treated in Ballesteros's more characteristic, serious vein in *Un incidente sin importancia* ("An Insignificant Incident," 1962), a distinctly Ibsenesque play, very reminiscent of *Pillars of Society*, about family guilt. The "incident" occurs when the son of the family pushes a girl, who had resisted his advances, out of a speeding car. The family lives in a provincial town not far from Madrid (the author himself, it should be remembered, lives in Toledo) and is desperately afraid of scandal. Its whole life seems to be a permanent tooth-and-nail struggle to present a false front to the world and to maintain its position just below the middle of the social ladder. The family's anxiety over the possible scandal brings various skeletons out of the closet; at the same time it stretches its habit of hypocritical subterfuge to the breaking point as its members clearly wish the girl would die before she talks. Ballesteros's character portrayal is masterly, particularly his picture of the son as a whining, self-pitying egoist, though his main point is excoriation of the community's rapacious pursuit of scandal and the pitiful, self-destructive entrapment of the family in its web of conformity.

Ballesteros's constant improvement as a theatrical artist and as a thinker is shown in two collections of plays, each consisting of four, essentially separate, one-act plays. These have recently established his reputation as one of the acknowledged leading writers of the new Spanish drama. *Farsas contemporáneas* ("Farces for Our Times," 1969)[6] won the Guipúzcoa Prize for 1969 and *Retablo en tiempo presente* ("Contemporary Altarpiece," 1969–70) won the prestigious Palencia Prize for 1970. While the plays in these two collections are independent as far as the specifics of their plots are concerned, they are intended to present the author's intellectual and satiric view of the world.

Farsas contemporáneas consists of four short plays, each with a descriptive subtitle: *La opinión* ("The Point of View"), against Violence; *Los esclavos* ("The Slaves"), against Consumption; *Los opositores* ("The Candidates"), against Classes; and *El hombre-vegetal* ("Vegetable Man"), against Conformity. In each of these Ballesteros has created a trenchant dramatic symbol that sums up a social evil. He has succeeded, in other words, in compressing the general into the specific without losing universal applicability. *La opinión* opens with an empty stage on which two actors debate on the function of the theater. The one, who is for theater as escape entertainment only, refuses to discuss anything rationally, simply broadcasting baseless dogmas with a bull-headed stubbornness that builds steadily to a blind rage. In his arrogance and stupidity he is a perfect caricature of the totalitarian mind. This "traditional" actor uses a ballerina to represent truth on the stage (or off), covering her from head to foot in a rose-colored garment. Then he pays policemen to beat the young "avant-garde" actor into submission (i.e., into saying that truth is rose-colored and not white, which he refuses to do). While beating the younger actor, the policemen speak of their duty and their responsibility to their families. The subtitle "Against Violence" is the same as saying "For Tolerance," and the play is an eloquent comment on the way tradition ossifies the mind and leads to brutality and corruption. The satire of the policemen and their hypocritical mouthings about obeying orders is, of course, standard stuff, though well done. It is in the use of the ballerina as the central symbol, representing at once the potential truth of art and the primacy of beauty, that the author shows his mastery.

In *Los esclavos* two ape-like couples sit picking fleas off each other and being hungry. A loaf of bread is lowered from the sky, and one of the couples grabs it, thus creating rich and poor by chance. The "rich" couple stop picking fleas and take off their ape masks. They are imitated by the other couple, whom they have to keep fending off in order to maintain their position. Finally they decide to make the starving couple produce bread in order to earn the money to buy it. This does not keep them busy all the time and leaves them time to think, so the rich advertise luxuries and status symbols. This converts the workers into veritable slaves, since they have to work constantly to produce more and more goods to earn the money to buy them. Simple-minded though this may sound in the retelling, it is not; for what Ballesteros has achieved here is the perfect form of the dramatic parable, in which it is necessary to compress and simplify without becoming sedulous and puerile. Ballesteros has managed to produce a history of the rise of consumer society from ape man to the contemporary age of the advertising huckster who creates an artificial need for conspicuous consumption.

In *Los opositores* Ballesteros has created a parable of the rise of

46

class society, which he sees as the result of the innate selfishness of man and of his longing for oblivion in a back-to-the-womb conformity. The candidates of the play are applying for status in a hypothetical mechanized society by taking a competitive test. Higher status goes to those who answer "don't know" to all questions; lower to those who attempt to solve the problems posed by the questions since this shows that they are curious, self-reliant, and "intellectually arrogant." The man who attempts to answer all the questions is condemned for trying to know everything and is relegated to the rank of third class citizen. He is advised to associate with second class citizens in order to improve himself. Second class citizens are, however, advised not to associate with third class citizens for fear of demeaning themselves. Ballesteros's depiction of the tenuousness of human relationships under pressure is particularly caustic. The candidates react like Pavlovian dogs to the commands barked out at them by the apparently omniscient loudspeakers, which not only tell them what to do but apparently are able to anticipate and predict what they intend to do. Thus, Ballesteros depicts men as willing to do anything for the security of an artificial social standing.

He treats a similar subject in *La colocación* (*The Position*),[7] part one of *Retablo en tiempo presente*. Here the position is obtained by personal influence rather than by an examination in which the correct attitude is not to have an opinion on anything lest one might harbor the potential for improvement (an injury to the sacred status quo). The principle is the same, however. Once one has the position, one is ensconced for life, one's chief duty being to fawn on one's superiors and abuse one's inferiors. Ballesteros's ever more effective use of dramatic symbolism here involves showing the candidate for the "position" being brought up to admire his mother's doll collection (since the life for which he is being prepared will be dull, quiescent, and non-productive) and to sit on barbs since enjoyment of life is a sin.

In *El hombre-vegetal*, part four of *Farsas contemporáneas*, Ballesteros deals with the necessity of fighting for freedom and progress, the greatest obstacle to which is the human vegetable who does nothing and just wants to live peacefully and not be involved (symbolized in the play by having him pay progressively larger sums of money for the privilege of occupying a rocking chair while the world disintegrates around him). What happens when such a man is forcibly brought out of his lethargy and deprived of the comfort he values above all else can be seen in *El héroe* (*The Hero*, 1965),[8] an ironic study of the myth-making process whereby "heroes" are created.

The Hero is the story of a man, José Kroll, who has been unjustly imprisoned for ten years, because he helped his fiancée and her brother—both, unlike himself, dedicated revolutionaries—to escape from the country. On his release, he is hailed as a hero by the revolutionary underground and is asked to flee the country himself. From abroad it is hoped he will be able to fight more effectively for the revolution. But Kroll is no hero—not even in an ironic sense. He is the average man who wants to live in peace, at no matter what cost to his self-respect and to his sense of justice. He is like an atom that has been ejected from the central mass to whirl around outside his regular orbit; and now he wants to return to the mindless inertia that is natural to him. Neither public ideals nor personal dignity mean anything to him. To his fiancée's brother, who comes to smuggle him out of the country to a hero's welcome in the revolutionary cells abroad, he reveals the fact that he manufactured evidence against innocent men while he was in prison simply in order to avoid torture. Finally, exasperated, he kills the brother in a blind fury and is hailed as a hero by the government that imprisoned him and now preens itself on brainwashing him from "revolutionary" to "hero."

José Kroll becomes a "hero" because he is called one. In the establishment of what we consider reality the superiority of the word over the act is the principal reason for the confusion between illusion and reality in our time. As Ionesco showed in *The Lesson*, semantic anarchy equals moral anarchy. When words are used to conceal facts and to determine the nature of the facts to be considered, life becomes false and destructive. Ballesteros treats this in two other parts of *Retablo en tiempo presente: La distancia* ("The Gap") and *El soplo* ("The Whisper"). In the former he applies the idea to love and marriage, showing a couple living together falsely entrapped by their faith in romantic words and visions of passion of the sort fed by pulp literature and popular song lyrics. In the latter he deals with the split between theory and action in religion. The same theme appears, as applied to war, in *Los peleles* (*The Straw Men*, 1968).[9] In this play Ballesteros comments on the way in which men are persuaded to fight each other on the basis of only minimally differing slogans.

Ballesteros has stuck to the same form of combining four thematically related satiric skits into a play collection in *Las estampas* ("Aspects," 1971). In *El superviviente* ("The Survivor") he contrasts the reality of political suppression, as told by the sole survivor of a massacre, with the lies reported in the newspapers. In *Los secuestros* ("The Hostages"), which is set in the Middle Ages, Ballesteros deals with the sort of political resistance represented by underground groups in sundry contemporary Latin-American countries, most notably Brazil and Uruguay, who kidnap prominent government officials in order to free their own men.[10] In *Las bicicletas* ("The Bicycles") Ballesteros uses the pointless pedalling of immobile gymnastic bicycles as an image for the pursuit of money for its own sake. And, finally, in *El orden chino* ("The Chinese Way") he deals with the arrogance of power in a play set in "the time of Buddha."

Los primates ("The Primates," 1971) is, unlike most of Ballesteros's recent work, a full-length play. As in *Los esclavos* he begins with prehuman characters wearing gorilla masks. But while *Los esclavos* was a capsule history of the rise of capitalism, *Los primates* is about the perversion of language and the hypocrisies that have grown up as a result. The two primates, male and female, are instructed by a Heavenly Voice in the uses of language, but from the very beginning the wrong associations are made between words, starting with the love-sin combination. From there Ballesteros proceeds to demonstrate his belief that all subsequent linguistic communication has been based on a perversion of truth and real relationships.

These latest plays of Martínez Ballesteros represent the maturity of his thought and artistic powers, and establish him as a powerful moralistic writer with a consistently humanistic viewpoint.

NOTES

1. A remarkably prolific author, Ballesteros wrote over twenty plays prior to 1960. These early plays are not considered here.

2. For *Football*, cf. *infra*, pp. 55–56.

3. Cf. *supra*, pp. 26–28.

4. Cf. my essay "La muerte del humanista: ensayo sobre el teatro de

Dürrenmatt, Hildesheimer y Bellido," *Revista de Occidente*, No. 93 (December, 1970), pp. 292–302.

5. Translated as *The Best of All Possible Worlds* by Henry Salerno and Sevilla Gross in *First Stage*, V, iii (1966) and in George E. Wellwarth, ed., *The New Wave Spanish Drama* (New York: New York University Press, 1970).

6. Published as No. 653 of the *Colección Teatro* put out by Escelicer (Madrid, 1970).

7. Translated by Robert Lima as *The Position* in *Modern International Drama*, IV, ii (Spring, 1971).

8. Translated by Robert Blue in George E. Wellwarth, ed., *The New Wave Spanish Drama* (New York: New York University Press, 1970).

9. Translated by Leon Lyday in *Modern International Drama*, III, i (Fall, 1969).

10. Bellido treats this theme more fully in *Rubio cordero*, cf. *infra*, p. 62.

4

JOSÉ MARÍA BELLIDO

José María Bellido Cormenzana was born in San Sebastián in 1922. In certain respects he is more fortunate than his fellow underground playwrights, although his efforts to live by his writing and to find sufficient free time for the practice of this profession have led him into the same material difficulties experienced by the others. San Sebastián, the capital of the Basque country, is only a few miles from the French border. Partly as a result of the contacts he made in his parents' resort hotel in San Sebastián and partly as a result of his university education (he holds a law degree from the University of Valladolid, though he has never practiced), Bellido learned English, French, Italian, and German. His linguistic abilities made it possible for him to earn his living for a period as a tour guide. More recently he has sold most of his interest in the hotel and has devoted himself exclusively to playwriting and translation.

The serious Spanish writer today is in a curious and anomalous position. In a sense the repression to which he is subject has made him more free than ever. The explanation of the paradox lies in the fact that once an author has resigned himself to the circumstances that prevail in Spain, he becomes absolutely free *within himself*. In a society where an author has some hopes of getting his works produced or published a certain degree of calculation is likely to creep into his work, perhaps unconsciously. The temptation to shape his writing to the exigencies of commercial production will always be there, and few are able to resist the small compromise here and there—very often an entirely harmless one—that will enable the work to be produced or published. The Spanish underground author has the cold comfort of being free of even the shadow of this temptation. In most cases he can be reasonably sure his play will not pass the censor. In many cases he does not even bother to submit it. To write for the theater of his own country is not his primary concern. Instead he writes for himself, for his friends, for the world. Spain and its socio-political situation are always a stimulus for him, but the plays are never exclusively about Spain. Spain is used as a microcosm of the world, because its problems are of immediate concern to the playwrights and because it differs from the rest of the world only in degree, not in kind. Spain is an intensification of the world; it is the world painted in starker colors. It is reactionary, but the signs are all too clear and ominous that it is where much of the rest of the world seems to be heading. The rest of the world still pays lip service to progress, but retrogression can look very much like progress if one has done an about face first. It is this false and illusory progress that the Spanish playwrights are in a unique position to observe and to warn against. "The government will not permit our plays to be published or produced, but what will we have to write about when the government changes?", one underground playwright once asked me. Like most Spanish remarks, this one contained a double irony, the unspoken one consisting in the fact that he knew that he would continue to have plenty to write about.

Despite their isolation, the best of Spain's playwrights have an extraordinary insight into the problems of the rest of the world. This is partly the result of the artist's instinctive sensitivity to the world, but for the most part the insights are concrete rather than instinctive. While many of the books that might give them these concrete insights are not available in Spain, and while the news that comes to them is printed in the government controlled newspapers, Spanish authors tend to be as well informed as anyone anywhere. To a considerable extent this can be traced to the government's reluctant capitulation to economic necessity in the late 1950's and the resultant rise of the tourist industry. Tourists are necessarily looked on with much the same deference and respect that the governments of the Central American republics used to show to the freighters and minions of the United Fruit Company. As a result, an enormous amount of information, both verbal and printed, has entered Spain, effectively counteracting the government's avuncular desire to confine the people's knowledge to what is "good" for them and nothing else.

Each of the leading underground authors has his own method of transforming this knowledge into dramatic terms. While there is nothing rigid or single-minded in the approach of any one of them, we have seen that José Ruibal tends to abide by his Galician heritage by inventing fantastic stories as his dramatic medium, and that Antonio Martínez Ballesteros displays a typically Castillian logic in the creation of his carefully constructed plays. José María Bellido's experiences have given him a cosmopolitan outlook, and his plays are each based on a central dramatic symbol. Bellido's plays frequently seem inchoate in comparison with Ballesteros's carefully structured works and they frequently seem static in comparison with the fast-moving plots of Ruibal's parables. What holds his plays together and makes the best of them the equal of any drama written today is his invention of dramatic symbols that encapsulate the preoccupations of our time.

Like the other Spanish underground playwrights, Bellido is extremely cynical. At first sight he seems to be a contemptuous *farceur* who reduces all life to the level of a ridiculous game sardonically observed from a superior viewpoint, much in the manner of Dürrenmatt. In Bellido, however, as in all of his colleagues, the cynicism is transmuted during the course of the play into optimism. Dürrenmatt can afford to be cynical and sardonic: he is free. To wallow in pessimism and hopelessness is the privilege of the untroubled. Solutions, which imply optimism, or, at the very least, the hint of dimly perceived gleams of light at the far end of the darkness, are a psychological necessity to those who are repressed. Paradoxically, then, our most optimistic writing comes from those who have least reason to feel hope, while our most pessimistic writing comes from those whose freedom from temporal pressures enables them to be dispassionate.

Bellido's principal themes are, inevitably, political and economic repression and the manipulation and exploitation by the few of the many. In his treatment of these themes he always concludes that the situation represents a temporary aberration and that the disparate elements of society will eventually be reconciled. This feeling takes on mystical proportions in *El pan y el arroz o Geometría en amarillo* (*Bread and Rice or Geometry in Yellow*).[1] Here he shows us a group of men representative of the power élite of society: a financial manipulator, a businessman, a landowner, a military officer, and a perverted intellectual. During a conference of these men, who meet in a timeless and imaginary setting, with a view to conquering the world, the intellectual "invents" patriotism, religion, propaganda, and money as a means of making people willing slaves of the power élite, under the impression that they are serving their own "freedom." Their plans, however, are upset by the mysterious appearance of a beautiful, smiling, yellow child during a sudden blackout. The blackouts begin occurring at seven minute intervals, and each time the number of children doubles. Meanwhile reports pour in that the whole city is inundated with these amiable and indestructible children. At the end, the rulers kill each other in their attempt to overcome the passive resistance of the children. With the device of the geometrically multiplying children Bellido conveys his faith in the efficacy of a Gandhi-like passive resistance, the sheer force of which causes the exploiters to kill each other in frustration. There is, unfortunately, a great deal of wish-fulfillment fantasy involved in this vision. It is only natural for a person brought up in a repressive society to gravitate toward visionary idealism, particularly when the society is surrounded by permissive societies. Gradually, however, Spanish authors are losing their faith in the social justice and the freedom that they associate with democratic society, because they see the societies they envy and admire becoming more and more like their own society and supporting it for politically pragmatic reasons. A second reason for loss of faith is their observation that their fellow-countrymen mysteriously lose their idealism and indignation as their lot becomes easier and their financial position more secure. The lust for freedom and the hatred of evil is not the universal emotion shown by Bellido with his indestructible and smiling children, symbols of benign solidarity.

As in all of the plays of the Spanish underground, there is no overt reference to Spain in *Bread and Rice*. One of the side effects of Spanish censorship has been to increase the scope of the Spanish drama and to force the authors to universalize their themes. Thus, by one of those perverse ironies that chroniclers of the inefficacy and bull-headedness of censors delight to record, the very existence of the censor has caused the wider dissemination of the Spanish drama and the transformation of what was potentially only a purely local drama into an internationally valid art form. A play like *Bread*

José Ruibal and Alfred G. Brooks (l. to r.) on the set during rehearsals for the world premiere of Ruibal's *The Man and the Fly*, directed by Brooks at the State University of New York, Binghamton, November, 1971. *Photo by Chris Focht.*

Jack Bradt as The Man in José Ruibal's *The Man and the Fly*, Binghamton, N.Y., November, 1971. *Photo by Chris Focht.*

Alfred Wilson as The Double in José Ruibal's *The Man and the Fly*, Binghamton, N.Y., November, 1971. *Photo by Chris Focht.*

Scene from *Tiempo de 98* by Juan Antonio Castro, Madrid, 1971. *Photo by Julio Wizuete.*

Scene from *Los peleles* (*The Straw Men*) by Antonio Martínez Ballesteros, Toledo, Spain, 1971.

Scene from *Los esclavos* (*The Slaves*) by Antonio Martínez Ballesteros, Toledo, Spain, 1971.

and Rice thus becomes a play about the mechanics of totalitarian oppression in general rather than a play specifically about repression in Spain. Bellido's depiction of totalitarianism is extremely trenchant and precisely analytical. He depicts it as a combination of an overriding profit motive that blots out all traditional human considerations, an irresistible attraction to a purely mischievous moral perversity, and a brutal and subhuman stupidity.

In *Fútbol* (*Football*, 1963),[2] the theme of exploitation resolved in a fervently hoped for reconciliation is already fully developed. Bellido sets his play in an imaginary village curiously similar to Spain: a sort of down-at-the-heels microcosm. Thirty years before, a civil war in the form of a football (i.e., soccer) match had taken place in this village. And now the winners lord it over the losers with their gleaming new uniforms and their shiny, bright soccer balls, symbols of a strutting *machismo*. The losers—crushed, poverty-stricken, dressed in threadbare uniforms, and bouncing degrading little rubber balls—nurse their grievances and hope for better days. Whenever they try to forget their loss and bolster their egos by carrying regular soccer balls, these are quickly and contemptuously deflated by the javelins of the police. All their hopes are pinned on a mystical prophecy that a divine referee will come and save them by reversing the disputed result of the fatal match. And they have one material hope, too. From the second generation of the team has come Zapatoni, the superstar, symbol of the latent strength and material potential of their village. And just as the tremendous industrial potential smoldering beneath the surface of Spain (where it has been kept untouched by the smugly complacent winners, who have been too busy preening and strutting and crowing over their fallen opponents for thirty years) is coveted by the two great opposing world powers, so, in the play, Nestor and Fani, caricatured Russian and American respectively, try to buy Zapatoni for their teams. Salvador, a traveling actor in costume, is mistaken for the "referee from the sky" of the prophecy, because he is wearing a football referee's uniform under a monk's cassock, costumes of roles he has to play the next day. Salvador becomes a parody of a Christ figure trying vainly to bring peace with his ineffectual Bible reading and humanitarian pleading. In collusion the leaders of the two football clubs agree to sell out their people; and Salvador is killed by a shot that could only have come from the church tower. Bellido deliberately leaves the origin of the shot ambiguous: it came from the direction of the church tower, but Fani enters with a rifle at the end. The members of the two clubs unite to fight for their freedom, for they cannot trust their leaders, the outside powers, represented by Fani and Nestor, or the Church, which has blessed their "football games" for so long.

Bellido himself has set the play to music, although it is just as effective without music. The use of the football game as a metaphor for national strife and the reduction of the subsequent enmity to a quarrel over the degree to which the balls everyone carries around are inflated, emphasizes the triviality of the conflict and puts it into the perspective it merits. Here, too, Bellido shows a faith in regeneration through the democratic process, represented by the common people, that we can now view only nostalgically. In his later plays Bellido realized more and more that the exploiters and the manipulators will remain the real rulers. The common people either prefer it that way, or become hopelessly fragmented, or use the democratic process only to find a new demagogue to relieve them of their responsibilities.

Disillusionment and cynicism must inevitably replace idealism in the work of the contemporary thinking artist. The idealism is passionately longed for and discarded with pain and anguish; but discarded it must be if the artist is to mature and bear witness to the world as it is, instead of frittering away his talent in conjuring up enchanted forests in which the nightmare of reality is transformed into the daydream of fantasy. As the new Spanish dramatists have emerged from the purely provincial concern with the faults of their own society that gave them their original impetus, they have become less hopeful. Convinced of the hopelessness of writing for a society that suppresses their work, they have turned to writing for the free societies that permit them to speak and they have become more pessimistic as they see that the freedom to speak is in itself no solution. Like the absurdists, they have replaced temporal hope with cosmic hopelessness.

Bellido's *Tren a F . . . (Train to H . . .*, 1964)[3] depicts an imaginary country which consists of a barren plain crossed by a train in which the inhabitants are traveling to H . . . , which could mean happiness, paradise, social progress, or everyone's private desires. All the passengers own shares in the railroad company (except, of course, the emaciated parodies of human beings stuffed into cattle cars at the rear of the train and let out only to chop the wood needed to keep the train going). Even so, the train, which is rickety and creaking in contrast to the streamlined diesels and buses streaking across the plain in the distance, frequently and inexplicably breaks down. When it does, the passengers sing hymns in praise of the railroad company and make obsequious remarks to the unctuous conductors and ticket inspectors, who reassure them, spy on them, or reprimand them, according to the occasion. As the narrator, an incipiently rebellious young man who wants to leave the train for more modern transportation, puts it, "trip after trip, century after century, that little train with its wooden cars, [stopped] for no apparent reason at improbable stations . . . lost in the immensity of the plain." What keeps the company in business is the belief of the passenger-shareholders that only the company's trains have access to the tunnel which is the only route to H . . . ; and, like one of the Church Fathers looking complacently down on the torments of the sinners in hell, they comfort themselves with the reassuring image of what they will see when they finally come to that tunnel which only the company can negotiate: "thousands and thousands of vehicles . . . smashed into smithereens, crashing into the mountain . . . gigantic mounds of twisted iron on all sides of the tunnel . . . And the moaning and groaning of the dying travelers who chose to ride with our competitors." This brilliant dramatization of the stultifying force of tradition, or religion, or political conservatism, or family (much of Bellido's skill lies in managing to allude to all of these while avoiding any specific references) is based on two central symbols.

Throughout the play the young man who narrates the story is torn between his desire to leave the rickety train, in whose ability to reach the tunnel he really has no faith, and the pleas of his mother that he return to the train and obey the rules laid down from time immemorial by the Company. The young man finally succumbs to this pressure and returns. Here Bellido's use of the Oedipus complex associates tradition, conservatism, and mindlessness with the psychological pull of family relationships. The triumph of the older generation in this eternal conflict symbolizes stasis and the inability of each new generation to break away from the Oedipal bond that keeps it imprisoned in the old order. Bellido's other principal symbol in this play is one he uses so often that it has become the central symbol in his thought. To Bellido the identifying characteristic of the life style that he satirizes and excoriates is the denial of time. The futile effort to halt the passage of time by submerging oneself in an ecstasy of self-delusion is a factor common to all systems of thought that worship tradition for its own sake, or that seek to justify a worn out and invalid power structure. In the play the station at which the train stops is dominated by a huge clock which has run down. The young man winds it up, but it is his last gesture before succumbing to the time-denying Oedipal pull. As the train pulls out on its futile, endless, and aimless journey, the clock will run down again, the train will return again, and the eternal cycle will be repeated with the next generation. The young man's last words as he helplessly embraces his mother are, "All that mattered was that I felt happy. Yes, I felt like a coward and—why not admit it?—sad! Sad because I knew I would never dare to leave the train again. Sad because I had renounced my dreams—my longings—my plans to change everything—renounced them forever."

While it is true that the denial of time is futile, it is futile only ultimately. Thus there is a tacit implication in Bellido's use of this symbol that those who attempt to halt time will fail. Nevertheless, on the purely socio-political level the attempt is completely successful, and in this way the spirit of the plays is cynical and hopeless. There is cold comfort in the knowledge that the officials of the Railroad Company are cosmically foolish since they are able to enslave the passengers within their own lifetimes.

Bellido employs the same symbolic theme again in *Los relojes de cera* ("The Wax Clocks," 1967), in *El día sencillo* ("The Easy Day," 1964), and in *Escorpión* ("Scorpion," 1962). *Los relojes de cera* takes place in an unspecified totalitarian country, in accordance with the invariable rule of the underground drama. As always in Bellido's plays, the plot itself is less important than the overall symbolic structure of the play. An inoffensive hotel owner in a seaside resort is constantly victimized by burglars—five robberies in one month—but as long as he seeks no redress he is at least free. When he finally reports the burglaries to the police, he is lost. The Police Commissioner who comes to investigate, significantly named Antofagos, already knows everything and is interested only in the aggrandizement of the State which he represents. When the hotel owner reminds him that years previously he was himself one of the revolutionaries responsible for putting the present government in power, Antofagos cynically points out to him that the structure of the State is always like oil and vinegar: separate levels. During a revolution the State is shaken up and the disparate elements are mixed together at random, but as soon as the revolution is successful and things quiet down again, the former levels return again as separate as ever. Bellido's view here is precisely the same as Genet's in *The Balcony* when he has Roger, the true revolutionary, realize in utter disillusionment that all revolutions are inevitably failures, since the rebellious victors instinctively institutionalize themselves as soon as they assume power in order to preserve their newly won position. Bellido does not, however, go as far as Genet, who concludes the necessity of constant revolution. The title of the play is a reference to the time symbolism. Bellido's imaginary country is a backward one, of course—just as backward now as it was before the supposedly beneficial change in government. Previously the country had been known as the world's leading producer of candles, but since the revolution—which was of the Communist type and therefore anti-religious—candles are no longer manufactured. The country's enormous supplies of wax are therefore used to make clocks, which have been put up at every street corner. In order to give the tourists, who now constitute the country's main industry, the illusion that time has not stood still there (as, in fact, it has), little yellow jeeps full of soldiers constantly scurry around moving the hands of the clocks. The wax clocks are symbols of life under totalitarianism, as the soldiers who move the hands are symbols of its pragmatic hypocrisy.

Escorpión is a play that is almost entirely composed of symbols. More than in any other of Bellido's plays, the plot is subordinated to the meaning transmitted through the symbols. In no sense, however, is this or any other of Bellido's plays an alphabet soup of symbols like Albee's later plays or like some of Tennessee Williams's, where recognizable literary symbols are thrown in at random without regard to their contextual relevance, only to impress unwary critics and awe naive viewers.

The significance of the title of Bellido's play is in itself purely symbolic. Bellido specifies that the curtain should have an enlarged reproduction of a scorpion painted or projected on it together with a scientific description of the animal. To Bellido the scorpion and the way it acts when threatened is a symbol of society today. The picture on the curtain is intended to set the tone for the rest of the play, since no further specific reference to the animal occurs. The plot itself is extremely simple: a delegation of various representative types from a small village visits the headquarters of a huge company in order to petition them to give up a project that will include the destruction of the village. The villagers obtain no satisfaction, of course. Indeed, they obtain no straight answers to their petition at all. Bellido's intention is to show the ordinary relationship between governed and governing in a typical democracy. From his original purpose of writing plays criticizing totalitarianism Bellido has progressed, if that is the word, to plays criticizing contemporary versions of democracy. The ironic power of the play does not become apparent until one realizes that it is, indeed, about the relationship between rulers and ruled in a democratic society.

Bellido introduces his time symbolism by putting the seat of government (the big company that proposes to destroy the village by flooding it while building a dam) in a museum, a place where time stands still and the mistakes of the past are exhibited in petrified horror as they are endlessly repeated with a kind of static stubbornness. Although the administration of the museum changes, the museum itself remains the same. The eight executives who pose, like paternal wax figures, above the action are replaced during the play by eight identical men, and Bellido implies that this process will go on *ad infinitum*. The rulers have always been of the same type: *plus ça change, plus c'est la même chose*. A change in government, Bellido is saying, is a change in store window dummies. He emphasizes this right at the beginning of the play, when the curtain rises to display the scene and is then immediately lowered again. There follows an entre'acte of a minute or so during which we hear the sounds of scene changing and the shouted instructions of carpenters and scene shifters. When the curtain rises again, the stage is *precisely* as it was before. Another aspect of the constant change of leaders is that one never knows who, ultimately, is really in charge: the President? the Chairman of the Board? the Council of Advisers? the *Eminence grise*? Or Someone even higher up who remains always invisible and inaudible, though immanent?

There are other symbols in the play, all illustrating aspects of the political power structure. There are two juke boxes on stage, one of them covered with a black cloth and candles so that it looks like an altar. This one does not work, though it takes money. The two acts of the play are entitled "Curiosity" and "Fear," those being the two chief methods by which people are kept in subjugation. If Curiosity does not work, Fear is used; but one way or another those in power, who are, of course, corrupted, maintain themselves at all costs and with complete cynicism.

Solfeo para mariposas ("Butterfly Song," 1969) is once again placed in a timeless setting. Bellido's principal concern here is war and its causes. To emphasize the timelessness of the problem and the ageless and unchanging nature of the causes of war he sets the play in a room which seems to represent the core of the Pentagon (or the Kremlin or the council chamber of Genghis Khan or of Mao Tse-Tung). Strictly speaking, it is an antechamber to the core, a waiting room outside the Holy of Holies from which the High Priest never emerges. Indeed, no one knows whether anyone is there at all. Everything is carried along by its own impetus, irresistibly impelled toward violence and evil. The *raisonneur* of the piece is dressed in eighteenth century clothes and accompanies his cynical remarks on a clavicembalo, in much the same way that Max Frisch emphasizes the timelessness of a similar problem in *The Chinese Wall*, where the *raisonneur* is dressed in modern clothes, while everyone else is in period clothes. The point here, as in Frisch's play, is that destruction is the be-all and the end-all of the inscrutable forces that govern humanity. There may very well be no one behind the mysterious door from which all orders seem to emanate, Bellido suggests. Everything is planned out of a love of pure evil by the desiccated old men in the outer room, men who are very much like those he portrayed as his symbolic power élite in *Bread and Rice*. Bellido uses sex symbolism here in an effective, paradoxical manner: as the desiccated generals watch the sinuous erotic movements of the dancing girls they have hired to strip before them they become re-inspired to put their projects of destruction into practice.

Bellido weaves his symbolism of sex and time into the fabric of his *El día sencillo*, in which a young man poses as a woman all year except for one day—the "día sencillo"—when he allows himself to revert to the manhood that a world that worships violence and devours its young men indiscriminately in one war or "police action" after another denies them.

In his more recent work, which includes some plays written frankly for the commercial theatre, Bellido has been turning away from symbolism and back to realism. The most outstanding example of this trend in his work is *Rubio cordero* (1970) [4] which was inspired by the recent rash of kidnappings of foreign diplomatic officials by Latin-American terrorists. In an unspecified setting, vaguely reminiscent of Uruguay, the local terrorist group kidnaps the Belgian ambassador in order to free their compatriots and to obtain funds for their continued operations. Bellido has by no means written a guerrilla theater tract with sharp divisions between good and evil. The moral conflict in the minds of the terrorists, who are all mild-mannered intellectuals that have, so to speak, been backed against the wall by their desperation in the face of brutal injustice, is shown with extraordinary skill. The scene in which the ambassador, who is completely in sympathy with the rebels, and the leader of the terrorists discuss their relative positions is the most mature exposition of the moral dilemma facing the revolutionary that we have in the modern drama. Bellido has put into dramatic terms what Joseph Conrad stated long ago in his preface to *Under Western Eyes*: "The ferocity and imbecility of an autocratic rule rejecting all legality and in fact basing itself upon complete moral anarchism provokes the no less imbecile and atrocious answer of a purely Utopian revolutionism encompassing destruction by the first means at hand, in the strange conviction that a fundamental change of hearts must follow the downfall of any given human institutions."

José María Bellido, together with José Ruibal and Antonio Martínez Ballesteros, is one of the three leading playwrights of the Spanish underground drama. They are the members of the older generation of the new movement whose efforts and pertinacity have encouraged their younger followers. Each has his distinctive style, Bellido with his symbolism, Ruibal with his parables, Ballesteros with his dramatized didactic essays. Each has had his influence, and their younger colleagues have taken from each whatever best suited the development of their own styles.

NOTES

1. Translated by Robert Lima in George E. Wellwarth, ed., *The New Wave Spanish Drama* (New York: New York University Press, 1970).

2. Translated by David Turner in Michael Benedikt and George E. Wellwarth, eds., *Modern Spanish Theater* (New York: E. P. Dutton & Co., 1968).

62

3. Translated by Ronald Flores in *Modern International Drama*, I, ii (1968) and in George E. Wellwarth, ed., *The New Wave Spanish Drama* (New York: New York University Press, 1970).

4. The title literally means "Fair-haired Lamb" and is a reference to the ritual slaughter performed before a Greek tragedy, to which the proposed slaughter of the ambassador is compared.

5

JUAN ANTONIO CASTRO

Juan Antonio Castro was born in Talavera de la Reina in 1927. Talavera is a small city in the extreme western part of the Province of Toledo near the dividing line between Castile and Extremadura, living on its past glories as the birthplace of Juan de Mariana and, above all, as the home of Fernando de Rojas, author of *La Celestina*. Historically, Talavera is practically a compendium of the Spanish past, since every wave of change that has contributed to Spain's development seems to have washed over it. It was captured by the Romans under Quintus Fabius Flaccus, by the Moors under Tariq, reconquered by Alfonso VI in 1082, and was the scene of the defeat of the French under Joseph Bonaparte by Cuesta and Wellington in 1809. Thus, Castro, like Ballesteros, comes from the very heartland of Spain. Like the Toledoan, he exhibits that hard and straightforward quality, that single-minded purity of purpose that is so typical of men from this part of the country, where the cultural and moral atmosphere has been least leavened by foreign influences. Urbanity, cosmopolitanism, and relativism are the qualities we can least expect to see in the Castillian writer, but this lack is balanced and more than compensated for by his characteristic quality of unwavering clearsightedness and his directness of approach.

  While their basic moral orientation toward their writing is essentially the same, Castro and Ballesteros differ in their immediate method. Where Ballesteros, as has already been noted, tends to write direct, symmetrically constructed dramatizations of moral,

64

political, and philosophical problems, Castro has two quite distinct styles: a wry, satiric humor in his short plays and a type of modern morality play in his longer ones. The morality play style is seen most clearly in two of Castro's three longer plays— *Plaza de mercado* ("Market Place," 1966) and *Era solo un hombre vestido de negro* ("There Was Only a Man Dressed in Black," 1968). In *Tiempo de 98* ("The Days of '98," 1969),[1] however, Castro uses the direct historical, chronicle form. In its structure the play is very close to Martin Duberman's *In White America*, which attempted to present a history of the subjugation of the Black man in the United States through the use of a collage of actual documents and testimonies recited by a group of actors each of whom took several parts. Using a very similar technique, Castro tries to give his audience a history of modern Spain in terms of its literary culture. The title of the play refers to the so-called "Generation of '98," five authors and their followers who brought about the re-vivification of Spanish literature in the last years of the 19th century, freeing it from the artificialities that had largely characterized it throughout the century and placing it in the mainstream of modern European literature, while retaining a distinctively Spanish quality. The five principal writers associated with this movement, whom Castro brings into his play, were Ramón del Valle-Inclán, Pio Baroja, Miguel de Unamuno, Azorín, and Antonio Machado. Because of their influence these men virtually formed twentieth century Spanish literature. Castro, however, is concerned not so much with their literary influence as with their moral influence—with their embodiment of all that is best in the Spanish character and with all that has remained uncorrupted. Castro's frame for the play is an elementary school history class in which the students recite the sad facts of nineteenth century Spanish history, most of them an illustration of political bull-headedness and ineptitude, social cynicism, frivolity, and misplaced and ill-timed patriotic fervor. Castro fleshes out this picture of Spain with two narrators, Alpha and Beta, who represent, respectively, enlightened liberalism and stubborn, unthinking reaction, and with a group of old men who comment on everything from the traditional viewpoint. Thus when one of the narrators announces that the Constitution of 1869 guaranteed freedom of education, the conversation of the traditionalists goes like this: "What an atrocity, Don Genaro!" "One of our dearest traditions is being trampled on." "You said it! Trampled on—and how!" The narrator interrupts to inform them that freedom of religion has also been instituted. "How barbaric, Don Genaro!" "Spain has always been the hammer of heretics." "Well said, yes, sir! The hammer of heretics!" The five writers, all of them played by the same actor, form the salutary antidote to this attitude. Their humanism is used as a contrast to the ostrich-like isolationism and provincialism as well as to the numb inflexibility of intellectual response prevailing in the Spain of their day. The implication that the work of the five authors is not complete and that the type of thinking represented by the reactionary characters in the play continues is, of course, clear, and it is reinforced by the contemporary setting—a class learning Spanish history. To anyone in the slightest degree familiar with the works of the "Generation of '98" there is something marvellously evocative in the straightforward quotations from their works that Castro sprinkles throughout the play. At the same time it becomes clear that Castro's intention in the play is to contrast the clear-sighted honesty of the writers, their insistence on the truth, however painful, with the perversity of those who say that all is well and that nothing should be changed. *Tiempo de 98* is probably the most thoroughly Spanish play of any of those treated in this book, based as it is on Spanish history and Spanish literary tradition, neither of them, unhappily, known extensively outside Spain. Nevertheless, it is a play of surpassing literary quality and one that would retain its force for an audience even only slightly acquainted with these two subjects, for the first is a primer of political errors and misgovernment and the other at least on a par with English, French, and German literature.

Castro's earlier full-length play *Plaza de mercado* is an allegorical satire on repressive officialdom and, as such, is much more in the mainstream of the Spanish underground drama, the grotesqueries consequent upon excessive government intervention in the private affairs of the citizenry being one of its principal and most frequently encountered themes. The play is set in the market place of a small town in South America or along the Mediterranean. Castro portrays the usual market place of such a town—colorful, bustling, and full of life. Almost immediately a sinister element is introduced, however, as a black-coated government functionary enters to buy a funeral wreath for his deceased office chief. His business is refused by the young flower seller, who asserts that she does not provide flowers for death. The functionary amiably gives her a piece of free advice: she is making a mistake—the future is in selling mourning flowers. His advice turns out to be only too apt since he is soon followed by two policemen who, with huge pens and enormous ink-wells, go around writing out summonses for those not possessing permits. They seal up the flower seller's stall and arrest her for not having any permits—there are permits for everything, even one for the right to bribe the officials to overlook the absence of other per-mits. A young man who has been making some silly remarks from the balcony of the hotel is arrested along with the flower seller, and the rest of the play turns into a satire on the repression of free speech with a mock trial in which the prosecutor suggests that the accused is *a priori* guilty because he speaks of individualism instead of duties to the state. The judge's charge to the jury warns them that any bias, one way or the other on their part, will be treated as a criminal act, but that since the accused is obviously guilty anyone voting for acquittal will himself be tried. Whereupon the jury marches out to its fore-ordained deliberations in military lock-step. The last act begins during the night preceding the execution of the young man who has dared to assert his individuality. The square is filled with amorphous shadows vaguely flitting about and whispering to each other all sorts of fantastic stories about the condemned man, showing how the populace is swayed and manipulated by the slight-est rumor. At the end the accused is beheaded while a radio com-mentator describes the scene as if it were a sporting event. This device almost succeeds in saving the last scene from melodrama, which, together with the sketchy characterization of the protagonist, marks this play as an apprentice work. However, the satire on bureaucracy and on justice, achieved through grotesque exaggera-tion, is as good as anything along these lines to be found in the mod-ern drama.

Castro abandons the specific and rather humorous satire of *Plaza de mercado* in *Era solo un hombre vestido de negro*. In this play Castro's criticism of society is much more radical. Again the scene is the central square of an unspecified town, but the resemblance to the previous play ends with the setting. Nothing is more likely to degenerate into triteness than the use of a Christ symbol, but Castro makes this the basis of this play and succeeds triumphantly. The characters, with the exception of the Mayor and the Man in Black, are all members of a Chorus of townspeople from which actors periodically step out to incorporate specific roles. The Mayor, as so often happens in Spanish underground drama, is a ruthless power figure pragmatically concerned with maintaining his supremacy at all costs and with subduing people by Machiavellian methods. Castro's portrayal is not a caricature. It is a thoroughly believable characterization and, despite the excesses of cynicism with which it is imbued, it is, unhappily, a completely realistic and not at all exclusively Spanish one. The mysterious appearance of a man dressed in black who has collapsed in the middle of the town square, apparently as a result of physical debility, is, on the surface, no threat to the power structure. But since the Man in Black is an unknown factor and not planned for in the system that the Mayor has erected, he must be treated as a potential threat. Anything unauthorized or that does not fit into the formulaic totalitarian conception of life must be eliminated or denied. And so the Mayor decrees that the Man in Black is simply not there—that there is a hole in space in the center of the plaza. Blinded by their preoccupation with power, the authorities can see nothing in the Man but a menace to their supremacy. The populace, however, is not immersed in the single-minded lust for power, which causes the creation of a distorted and unreal view, and thus it can perceive instinctively the true significance of the event. The suffering Man, dressed in black as a sign of mourning for the world, writhing in agony, and barely able to enunciate his message of universal love, is recognized as a Messianic apparition. But the members of the Chorus, who now assume, with the aid of masks, the form of all the races of the world, reject the Man and his message. After two thousand years of suffering and evil, of cruelty and inhumanity, the Second Coming is inadequate, feeble, and too late. After the atrocities and the bestialities, after the wars and the genocides, the message of Christ has become contemptible and puerile. The Man in Black is rejected and his impractical admonition ignored. For a short time, while the authorities observe the reaction to Him and ascertain that He will not be accepted, He becomes a tourist attraction: religion becoming commercialized for politico-economic reasons. But even here He is inadequate, for nobody is interested in coming to see a void, which is what Castro suggests religion has become. Finally, rejected by all, the Man in Black is condemned by the Chorus in a ritual chant and is crucified: "four men stretch the condemned man out on the ground. They nail his hands and feet to the ground with a large hammer. At first this action has a ceremonial and ritualistic air, but gradually the four executioners become more and more excited. The

Chorus, too, becomes animated and eggs the four on. The final beats of the hammer should have a demented rhythm while the Chorus, breathing hard in an almost obscene manner, goes into paroxysms." The moment this climax is reached, the Chorus becomes a group of tourists again and one of them becomes the guide showing the others around. In a trenchant commentary on the unreality of society, not only as depicted in the play, but outside it as well, the "guide" shows the "tourists" the theater and the audience sitting in it, thus drawing the spectators and the lives they lead into the vortex of unreality—the denial of truth—exemplified by both the Mayor, with his dream of a society of human robots subservient to him, and by the Man in Black with his dream of a cloudy Utopia where all problems will be solved by all men automatically loving each other.

Castro's other style of playwriting is shown in a series of his short plays, chief of which is *La visita* (*The Visit*, 1970),[2] a hilarious imitation of absurdist drama that reads like a take-off on Ionesco's *The Bald Soprano*. His *Diálogos docentes* ("Instructive Dialogues," 1967) are a series of very short sketches or "black-outs" that make wry commentaries on human foibles, as in the following one on "Liberty":

ALPHA: The freedom of your fists ends where my nose begins.

BETA: In other words, my fists are free up to an inch from your nasal appendage?

ALPHA: No, because that would limit the freedom of my nose to only an inch.

BETA: How about a foot?

ALPHA: That's no good either. That would be a clear provocation, a threat. Provocation and threat are hardly different from the act and the injury.

BETA: So where does the freedom of my fists end?

ALPHA: In your trouser pockets.

BETA: And of yours?

ALPHA: At the trigger of my gun.

Juan Antonio Castro has developed more slowly than the other underground authors of his generation. The number of his works is too small to enable us to trace his development as a writer. As a result he appears to have progressed by leaps, going from the uncertainty of *Plaza de mercado* directly to the depth and maturity of *Tiempo de 98* and *Era solo un hombre vestido de negro*, the former a play that affirms his faith in a Spain that can produce men like the Generation of '98, the latter a masterpiece of cynical commentary on the modern world written in a poetic language and with an unflinching straightforwardness that makes him a worthy disciple of his literary heroes.

NOTES

1. Juan Antonio Castro, *Tiempo de 98* (Madrid: Escelicer, 1970).
2. Translated by Patricia O'Connor in *Modern International Drama*, V, i (1971).

6

JERÓNIMO LÓPEZ MOZO

Jerónimo López Mozo is the most prolific of the younger generation of the Spanish underground drama. Born in Gerona, in the
extreme northeastern part of Spain near the French border in 1942,
he makes his home now in Madrid, as do virtually all of Spain's
dramatists, unless they are bound to provincial cities by family ties
or unless they choose to live in Barcelona, either for business reasons or because of their commitment to Catalan life and culture.

Despite the fact that López Mozo's job as a traveling salesman
takes him all over Spain and gives him ample opportunity to collect
material for an essentially indigenous Spanish drama, he writes primarily in a supranational vein. I have already commented on the
fact that the opening up of Spain through its forced reliance on the
tourist industry has made its authors increasingly conscious of the
fact that the problems afflicting their country are not peculiar to it,
and the cultural oppression to which they are subject fades into
comparative insignificance when contrasted with the inhuman oppression so rampant in the rest of the world. It becomes difficult to
write about oppression in one's own country when one contemplates
oppression in the world as a whole. Indeed, it becomes self-indulgent.
Nevertheless, in Spain it may be as difficult to write internationalist
drama as it may be in Greece, Brazil, or Russia, since what is true
of the macrocosm is inevitably true of the microcosm. And, if, by
chance, there should be no directly discernible relationship (as, for
example, in plays dealing with the racial problem) the innate para-

noia of the censor is sure to imagine it. López Mozo himself has put it this way, "When I write I try to forget the existence of the censorship and that our theater is condemned, for various reasons, to be known only by a very limited number of people. I still continue to write deliberately ignoring—to the extent to which they can be ignored—these obstacles, perhaps because my economic independence permits me to." This might as easily be spoken as a credo by any other of the Spanish underground authors, except that very few are blessed with the same degree of economic independence.

López Mozo has experimented in several styles: the cabaret revue, absurdism, and the historical, chronicle play. Whatever his style, however, his motivation is always the same. The principal feeling that informs López Mozo's plays is outrage. Where the older authors tended to be more dispassionate and to analyze, the younger ones tend to express an instant emotional reaction. Shock and its consequent disillusionment, a sense of outrage at the failure of the world outside Spain to measure up to the hopes that they have built up for it, is endemic in most of their plays. Frequently this feeling is so intense that a tone of stridency enters a play, but usually it is well under control. An instructive comparison might be made between López Mozo's plays on the violence that pervades the world and Megan Terry's. In the young contemporary American playwright's *Viet Rock*, for example, the stridency takes over almost completely. López Mozo does not make the mistake, so common in the contemporary American drama, of letting subjective emotionalism take over or of attempting to involve the audience in the action of the play. He seems to have sensed instinctively that an audience resents being drawn into the action of a play and that a far greater effect, both emotional and didactic, can be achieved through objectivity. It is in the audience's recognition of its own unconscious repressed attitudes in those displayed by theatrical characters that the playwright achieves his most trenchant effects. Attempting to make the audience participate is self-defeating, since it only stimulates resistance in its mind. Public confession is the outlet of the insincere and stupid. Purgation is a form of self-indulgence. Only by forcing a private recognition on the audience has the playwright any hope of bringing about a moral metamorphosis.

We can see López Mozo's skill in this technique in *El retorno* ("The Return," 1968), which, by one of those flukes that occasionally occur in Spain, has been passed by the censorship office, though it has not as yet been produced outside university theaters. *El retorno* contrasts self-indulgent insensitivity with agonized sensitivity in the face of the atrocities committed by human beings on each other. A young man tries to communicate to two other young people the anguish and guilt aroused in him by his contemplation of the agony suffered by the human race at its own hands. But the two others, male and female, while fully aware of all the things troubling their companion, cannot be bothered, and beg him to leave them in peace and stop depressing them with his all too-obvious despair so that they can discuss more important things, such as where and how to spend their vacations. The characters are constantly merging and exchanging roles. Thus Pipo, Mosca, and Bruno become merely names for anyone at all. The technique López Mozo uses here is similar to that originated independently by the Brazilian director-playwright Augusto Boal at the Arena Theatre of Saõ Paulo. Boal's so-called "joker" technique tries to show, by rotating the actors in their roles, that the human agents of the actions are unimportant *per se*, and that social forces cause historical events. Thus in López Mozo's play the sensitive Pipo immediately becomes insensitive to the misery of the world when Mosca turns her attentions from Bruno and seduces him. The individual's attitude is determined by outside forces.

El retorno is essentially naïve—a young man's play—ending with an affirmation that quiescence in the presence of injustice is a sin, and only protest, however baffled, is morally valid. This is an attitude typical of a moral man in a repressed country, who finds it hard to accept the disillusioning fact that countries he admires as being free are basically as immoral and callous as his own. The play is an unbelieving protest by a young author against what he is just realizing is true.

By the time he wrote *Collage Occidental*, which won the *Premio Nacional de Teatro para autores universitarios* in 1968, López Mozo realized that it indeed is all true. The play, as the title indicates, is a series of scenes depicting the malaise of the Western World. Despite the fact that the play was awarded a national prize, it did not pass the censorship, a fairly common occurrence in Spain, which is nothing if not a land of paradoxes. The situation is not, indeed, unusual, and it is not without reason that the Spanish underground authors are fond of referring to themselves with cynical self-deprecation as the authors with the most prizes and the least productions in the world.

Collage Occidental deals episodically with various ailments of the Western World today. The subjects range from politics, economic determinism, and restriction of personal liberty to love and eroticism. The episodes are connected by collages of movies and stills depicting elements of the scene that follows. The unifying image of the play is the personal conflict of Hache and his relationship with Eme.[1] Hache commits suicide in despair at the isolation of man and his inability to do good. Eme reads the diary he has left behind, and the various scenes show the situations that have driven him to his act. There are eleven collages in all, seven of which are particularly interesting. The first collage is preceded by images of huge crowds—mass meetings, political rallies, football matches, etc.—with a solitary man superimposed over them. This is followed by a scene in a circus with Hache as the pathetic clown figure, an image of man's solitude in the midst of his fellows. The second scene deals with wife-swapping as an image of the boredom and casualness of marital relationships. Again the emphasis is on isolation, though here it is isolation within intimacy rather than within the mass. The third scene is set in an insane asylum. Here López Mozo takes the theme of isolation one step further, showing the isolation of the human being from himself. The fifth scene uses a zoo as a symbol of human slavishness. The ideal of human freedom is depicted as an impossible one because men do not desire it and they resent and fear it when it is preached to them or when they see it in others. The security of the cage, and the zoo's regular daily feeding hours or the security of crawling about with a leash around one's neck, held by a power figure reminiscent of Pozzo in Beckett's *Waiting for Godot*, is far preferable to the uncertainty and aimlessness of self-responsibility. When the Pozzo-like character is killed, he is immediately replaced. When the cages are opened, the men refuse to come out. In the tenth scene religion is treated as a branch of the zoological/social order that encourages mankind to remain caged and leashed, subject to the financial exploitation with which López Mozo links religion by showing a priest wearing a heraldic device consisting of a clergyman rampant on a field of gold. The eleventh and last scene of the *Collage* is the scene that breaks Hache's spirit and drives him to suicide.

It is a scene that depicts political torture and can be interpreted symbolically as well as literally. Hache is in the hands of three torturers who have orders to make him say "Yes"—to acquiesce. The scene is reminiscent of Kafka, Ionesco, and Adamov. Hache is the rational man in an irrational world, the man that Ballesteros makes his hero. He wants to know to what he is supposed to acquiesce and at whose orders, but the torturers, mere functionaries who know nothing and care less, cannot tell him. Like Kafka's K, Hache is accused of no specific crime. He has only to say "Yes"—a symbolic answer with no reference to any particular question, but simply a general affirmation and acceptance of whatever is and an abdication of personal responsibility and individuality:

FIRST TORTURER: Maybe you don't quite realize the possibilities that'll open up for you if you say "Yes."

SECOND TORTURER: In the first place you'll be able to leave this room and go back free to your home.

THIRD TORTURER: You'll keep your job.

FIRST TORTURER: And besides they'll promote you. You'll be the boss. You'll earn more.

SECOND TORTURER: You'll never be bothered.

THIRD TORTURER: You'll have lots of other possibilities open up for you too.

FIRST TORTURER: We'll testify that your conduct is irreproachable.

SECOND TORTURER: That's just some of the nice things that'll happen to you if you say "Yes."

On a far more sinister level this is very like the submission to convention demanded of Ionesco's Jack. But Hache refuses, and progressively, with expressions of profound regret, the torturers castrate him and cut off his arms and legs. Finally, they rip out his tongue. Maimed and helpless, Hache is at last "free," for he can no longer say "Yes." He ends up the way Adamov's *Le mutilé* ends up in *La grande et la petite Manoeuvre* or Beckett's living torso in *The Unnamable*. All that Hache can do now is think, the only freedom left. The whole play, however, is in the form of a flashback after Hache's suicide and is a dramatization of the thoughts he has set down in his diary during his last days. His only hope of salvation has been in his relationship with Eme. But Eme—a modern, more determined, and tragic Lysistrata—has decided to give up love because of her feeling that children must not be brought into a world characterized by insincerity and war. Her attitude links the play with *La renuncia* ("The Renunciation," 1966), in which López Mozo wrote of a newly wed couple who decide to renounce sex in order to prevent the birth of further children. The couple is described as "neither young nor old; neither tall nor short, neither fat nor slim. . . . They are like everyone else." It is an early play and belongs to López Mozo's apprenticeship, the theme being more maturely treated in *Collage Occidental*. The trouble with *La renuncia* is that the prologue seems to indicate that the renunciation of sex is motivated by the evil of the world, whereas its subsequent development is more related to the couple's worries over their inability to predict what kind of children they would have.

Having dealt with the effect of war on the individual in *El retorno*, *La renuncia*, and *Collage Occidental*, López Mozo turns his attention to what he perceives as the causes of war in *Crap, fábrica de municiones* ("The Crap Munitions Factory," 1968), a play that is, of course, censored. His view occupies a middle ground between the simplistic one of Robert E. Sherwood's *Idiot's Delight* and the rational one of Shaw in *Major Barbara*. The style is Brechtian, with songs and presentational scenes. Crap's (the name is obviously reminiscent of Krupp) is an enormous munitions factory, whose owner practices the same sort of benevolent capitalism as Shaw's Undershaft. Shaw sees his manufacturer as a pawn in the game of capitalism, a link in an economic chain forged by historical forces, and makes a dramatic character out of him by making him recognize this. López Mozo adulterates his character somewhat by endowing him with diabolic manipulative powers. The play opens with a chorus of workers chanting self-abasing praise of their enslavement and of their pride in being associated with power: "The House of Crap is our second mother./It feeds fifty thousand families . . ./ Its fall would cause the greatest economic disaster in the history of the country. . ./Mr. Crap is more important than the President and one gesture from him would cause the government to fall." This is followed by a film showing the rise of the Crap organization since the time of Napoleon. Then the Crap Board of Directors discusses the unfortunate consequences of the very active and effective peace movement, concluding with a snappy song in which we are told that war has relatives: industry is its sister and the economy its blood brother. Crap decides that, in order to maintain the prosperity of the House of Crap and all who depend on it, he must start a war, which he will do by giving away arms for a whole year to small nations that cannot afford to pay for them in order to stimulate a greater conflagration. Crap goes, disguised as a poor salesman, to an underdeveloped country to instigate a revolution. As a result of his efforts, his business prospers again, but a great many people are, of course, exiled or otherwise rendered homeless. López Mozo presents a fine scene here, as he shows a chorus of exiles with the words Hungary, Korea, Algeria, Katanga, Yemen, Suez, Angola, Biafra, Vietnam, and Czechoslovakia written on their backs as they exit. At the end Crap and his associates are tried and condemned for crimes against humanity, but the judges decide it would be unwise to destroy Crap's factories since it would be perfectly safe to allow them to continue under strict supervision. There is no longer any danger of their products being misused, after all, since peace pacts have been signed. The judges, who have been masked during the trial, are revealed at the end as the politicians who have appeared throughout the play, though it is not clear whether we are to consider them to be constant dupes of the industrialists or as their active collaborators. Stylistically the play is perhaps the best imitation of Brecht that we have. Philosophically it is extremely simplistic, but no more so than Brecht's own single-minded ideological approach. Shaw and Ibsen realized that, given the complexities of modern society with its myriad interlocking parts, we can only ask questions.

The plays discussed so far have all been imbued, in one way or another, with indignation at injustice and they constitute a dramatic chronicle of a sensitive man's awakening to what Antonin Artaud called the cruelty of the world. Other plays of this type that López Mozo has written are *Matadero solemne* (1969),[2] an attack on capital punishment, which remains censored, of course, and *Blanco y negro en quince tempos* ("Black and White in Fifteen Scenes," 1967), a series of revue skits skilfully satirizing a number of social foibles. The author has not even bothered to submit this play to the censors. López Mozo has, however, also written plays specifically about Spain. In this he differs from the majority of his colleagues, who see no point in writing directly about Spain, since such plays have not the remotest chance of passing the censorship. Obliquity has been forced on the Spanish underground playwrights. López Mozo has chosen to break this mold by writing about the Spanish Civil War, realizing that that conflict was a paradigm for the violence and inhumanity of our times. In *Guernica* (1969) he tried to re-create in the audience the emotion of reliving the bombardment of the Basque city in 1937, the trial run for the "scorched earth" bomb-ings of World War II and Vietnam. This play is purely a scenario for performance. It means very little when read only. *Guernica* is multi-media, audience-participation theater of fact. López Mozo uses Antonin Artaud's concept of the three hundred and sixty degree stage with revolving seats for the audience and sufficient space be-tween the seats for parts of the action to take place. The seats are surrounded by screens. Each spectator is given a program and a candle. The actors enter carrying pieces of Picasso's painting, which they put together like a huge jig-saw puzzle on a screen at the back. After this the bulk of the play consists of an impressionistic re-creation by means of sound effects and photographs flashed simul-taneously on the five screens surrounding the audience. A fine theatrical effect is achieved at the end when all the actors light a candle and pass the fire on to the audience as the lights go out. López Mozo is an eclectic playwright in the best sense of the word, but here I think the influence has been unfortunate. The current movement toward audience-participation theater, toward attempt-ing to reproduce the emotions of the original event in each succes-sive performance, is based on a psychological error. The truth of the matter is that people are not moved by suffering—they revel in it. Mass suffering produces a prurient interest in people. They may be fascinated, horrified, repelled, and/or angered—but their emo-tions, the classic emotions of pity and terror, are not engaged. The bombardment of Guernica, no matter how realistically reproduced, no longer has any effect on them. It is too far in the past, and the suffering is too anonymous. Audiences are not moved by Guernica. They are not moved by Auschwitz, by Dachau, by Babi Yar, by Lidice, by Mylai. They are not moved—period. We have been bru-talized too much. Atrocities have become too commonplace to affect us anymore. The point of no return in human emotion has been reached. Sanity cannot comprehend the mass *autos-da-fé* of our perverted beliefs. People are moved privately by their personal tragedies, but these induce self-pity only. Publicly they can be moved only by phony emotion. Tears flow in rivers for the Lady of the Camellias, but not for reality.

The error of *Guernica* is avoided in López Mozo's most recent play, *Anarchia 36* (1971). This is a straightforward, chronicle play, using factual sources, often quoting actual speeches. The subject is the tragically divisive tri-partite conflict within the Republican side in the Civil War, between Anarchists, Communists, and supporters of the government itself. *Anarchia 36* is wholly successful where *Guernica* fails because it presents its subject purely objectively. The spectacle of the downfall of the Republic, not so much as a result of defeat by external forces but as a result of the welter of internecine strife among its own factions, is true tragedy. It is a spectacle that moves because it generates its own emotion rather than trying to induce it in the audience. The contemplation of the wilful destruction of an ideal through factional strife and the demonstration that the strife had reached an impasse, which is López Mozo's subject, constitutes true tragedy and produces the sadness and cynicism that are the natural emotional results of that genre.

López Mozo has made only one excursion into the absurdist style, in which he was heavily influenced by Ionesco, *El testamento* (*The Testament*, 1968).[3] In this play an old couple are spending their last night in a hotel room from which they will be summoned for their last journey in the morning. They are quite resigned, unafraid, and only concerned that they be remembered with respect. To this end they have composed a self-glorifying testament which they pass on to their grandson. The old couple think they are fooling their grandson and convincing him of their virtue, which they attribute to their unbending conformity to the ideals passed down to them. But the younger generation, López Mozo implies, is no longer fooled. While the old people are indulging in their orgy of self-praise, the grandson quite coolly reminds them of their former devotion to "Uncle Adolf" and "Uncle Benito," whose pictures they have now burned. As the old people die, the grandson, quite unemotionally, burns the testament.

Jerónimo López Mozo has clearly shown himself in these plays to be one of the foremost experimenters in contemporary Spanish drama, always searching for new themes and new techniques, and always developing into a more and more competent playwright. He is a writer of whom it may well be said without the slightest irony that his eclecticism is his strength.

1. "Hache" is the Spanish equivalent of "H," which here stands for *Hombre*—Man; "Eme" is the Spanish equivalent of "M," which here stands for *Mujer*—Woman.

2. It is difficult to make sense out of this title in English. It literally means "Solemn Slaughter House."

3. Translated by Alex Olynec in *Modern International Drama*, IV, i (1970).

7

MIGUEL ROMERO

Miguel Romero was born in Córdoba in 1930. At present he works as a publisher's editor and reader in Madrid. Although he has been neither published nor produced in Spain, Romero has attracted some attention in Germany, where his plays will be produced in the near future. Like his fellow underground writers, Romero feels that a writer must write what he feels impelled to write, and if what he writes cannot be produced, so much the worse for the theater. This is not to say that his plays are flaming revolutionary tracts. Quite the contrary. Romero's troubles with the censorship probably stem quite as much from his unbridled Rabelaisian humor and from the congenital supercautiousness of the censorial mind, whenever it is faced with something beyond its limited understanding, as from any overt political references. The references are there, certainly, but they are well hidden, and, as with most of the Spanish underground writers, they are not primarily or specifically references to Spain. In banning Romero's plays the censors are, as usual, chasing chimeras or looking over their shoulders at spectres conjured up by their own paranoid imaginations. Like all writers worth the name, Romero writes about the human condition, not about any specific grotesque manifestation of it. At the same time he is obliged to use his own experience of the human condition as a paradigm; and the unavoidable fact is that the paradigm becomes more distorted and unnatural in direct proportion to the lack of freedom under which it suffers.

Unlike his fellow writers, Romero writes neither in allegories nor in parables; and while he makes copious use of symbols, he cannot be classified as an essentially symbolic writer either. Romero's work is, indeed, unique and defies classification. His first two plays are enormously long and diffuse and seem to be totally formless and disorganized.[1] Yet a careful examination shows that this impression of vagueness is deceptive and that the plays are in fact enormously complex structures composed of many overlapping layers of text and full of multifaceted allusions. Where the relationship between text and meaning consists of a one-to-one substitution in allegory or a substitution of the whole by another whole in the parable, in Romero's plays the relationship is more like that between a root and the tangle of coiled tendrils it shoots forth.

The extraordinary complexity of Romero's work is partly accidental and partly deliberate. Frequently the richness of his imagination transports him into virtuoso flights of almost surrealistic grotesquerie, in which the core of his meaning becomes temporarily obscured by the convolutions and convulsions of his savagely mordant vision of life. The savagery is reminiscent of Ghelderode's tortuous vision of mankind as a swarm of corrupt and debased monstrosities snapping and snarling at the rare decent individual among them and finally overcoming and destroying him. Humanity is seen as a host of endlessly vermicular moral corkscrews. Combined with this acidulous view of the world there is an endlessly imaginative Rabelaisian ribaldry that raises Romero's vision out of the slough of pessimistic brooding in which Ghelderode's is mired. Through this frank and earthy humor he affirms his belief in human possibilities.

The other characteristic of Romero's work is wholly deliberate and involves a linguistic complexity that is as difficult to explain as it is essentially untranslatable. These linguistic distortions are the very framework of Romero's plays. He himself characterizes his plays as a Theater of Derision and explains that he obtains his effects through a union of high-flown literary language with slang, colloquialisms, and scatology. By means of a subtle juxtaposition of noble concepts and debased words he achieves a systematic degradation of the concepts, in order to deride the essential hypocrisy motivating his characters. Another device that he employs is obsessive repetition of sentences or parts of sentences so that the words lose their meaning, and the dialogue assumes a nightmarish, psychotic quality expressive of the inner emptiness of the characters. Still another linguistic device Romero uses frequently is the pun, usually playing on a word's formal meaning and on its vulgar meaning to achieve a sort of instant internal derision.

We can best see how Romero has worked out this extremely complex approach by looking directly at his plays. In *Patética de los pellejos santos y el ánima piadoso* ("Lament of the Saintly Dried-up Skins and the Pious Soul," 1970) Romero begins his linguistic tricks in the title itself. By introducing the connotatively ugly word *pellejos* into the series of noble-sounding words composed of "lament, saint, pious, and soul" Romero attempts to mock and degrade the concepts referred to by the words. A touch of Romero's characteristic mordant cruelty is achieved by substituting the expected word *piel* (skin) with *pellejos* (dried-up, wrinkled skin or peel). There is also an untranslatable political connotation involved, since *pellejos* is used colloquially in Spain to refer to dried-up, puritanical old people, hence reactionaries. The subtlety of the title is typical of the tortuous system of linguistic allusions and complex symbols that Romero builds up, both in this play and in *Pontifical* (1968). And although the full intricacy of his labyrinth of meanings may be lost under the swirls of baroque-like decoration with which he has overlaid it, the wit, humor, and inventiveness of the plots are in themselves sufficient to hold the interest of reader or spectator. Furthermore, the essential core of his meaning becomes clear through the characterization—much of it extremely skilful psychological parody —and through the satire implicit in the speech patterns that Romero constructs.

Patética is set high up in the Himalayas, where two disciples wait for their guru to return from his fasting and meditation in the mountains to show them the way to perfection. While they wait, endlessly repeating reassurances that he will indeed come to bolster their waning faith, the two disciples, a young man and a young woman, prepare the elaborate "stew of the saints" (another example of Romero's mocking fusion of linguistic incongruities) for their guru's refreshment. When he comes, however, he is so weakened by his fasting that he is killed by the shower of sunflowers with which his disciples joyfully greet him. The tableau of the guru expiring underneath the mound of sunflowers that his disciples have deliriously thrown at him is the first of a series of fantastically macabre scenes riddled with a desperate hilarity that make this play a supreme example of black humor in the modern theater. When they find that they have inadvertently killed their beloved guru, the two feckless disciples decide to show their reverence for him and for his teachings by pickling his body in a large jar of vinegar, so that he may always be with them in the flesh as well as in the spirit. Their choice of vinegar as the pickling substance is, in itself, a tribute to the late guru, for he was known in life as the Vinegar Guru because he distributed the acrid fluid wherever he went, as a sign and a warning that life is not easy and that the path to virtue is beset with hardship. Unfortunately, the late guru was so emaciated, as a result of his constant fasts, that his cadaverous head, streaming vinegar, keeps bobbing over the lip of the jar as his wasted body floats to the top of the pickling fluid, much to the discomfiture of the two disciples. They now see their only hope in the Guru of Gurus, and when he finally arrives the two disciples hasten to offer themselves to him as his followers. The Guru of Gurus turns out to be an intensely unpleasant person, unlike the dead man, who, though he preached the Way of Vinegar, was extremely mild and gentle. According to the Guru of Gurus, a much more modern evangelistic hell-fire and brimstone type, the dead guru was an anachronism who always insisted on pouring his drop of vinegar into everything. At this point the clean, sharp edge of Romero's meaning begins to cut through the tangled skein of ribaldry in which he has wrapped his play. The new guru is an obvious hypocrite and a sleek, commercialized version of the real thing. His specialty is obfuscation, and his diatribe against the late guru's predilection for vinegar makes it clear that the vinegar (which is now preserving the guru and will continue to preserve him) represents truth, reality, or uncompromising honesty. To the false but grandiosely titled Guru of Gurus these things are anathema, of course, and he launches into an almost hysterical denunciation of vinegar, saying that it poisons stews, meals, social life, everything: "And it is precisely thus that the ways of perdition begin—with a few drops of vinegar. Not one single drop of vinegar is permissible—not one single drop. And he wanted to achieve perfection by the paths of vinegar—that's what he wanted. . . . And he ignored the fact that vinegar irritates the taste buds, that it irritates the skin [*pellejos* is used again] of the palate. And that in this sense vinegar is masochism, pure masochism. . . . And masochism is not the way to perfection, that it is not. Your guru walked the ways of perdition. . . . May God have mercy on his soul." The Guru of Gurus' substitute for vinegar turns out to be sugar—and specifically, commercially refined sugar. The symbolic contrast between the two gurus and the Ways they preach now becomes obvious. The whole ribald and fantastic fable about these Oriental gurus and their devoted disciples stands revealed as a fiendishly clever satire on modern Christianity and political totalitarianism, as the Guru of Gurus intones a prayer in praise of the Holy Angel of Thinking About Nothing and the Holy Angel of Thinking As Little As Possible. Progress is decreed to be a sacrilege and a profanation by the Great Guru, because everything is already perfect and it is blasphemy to suppose anything else. At this point—in a scene of unequalled macabre hilarity—the guru in the vinegar revives (the last gasp of truth?) and has to be definitively disposed of by his rival who sits on top of the pickle jar and presses him down. A more mordant image of the suppression of truth by the bland assumptions of arbitrary and pragmatic authority could hardly be imagined. The Holy Guru then formulates—on the spot—the doctrine that all holiness lies in the skin, so that he can caress the girl disciple, but, more faithful to the old guru than the boy, she rebels. In a frenzy the Guru of Gurus tries to stab her, but her companion throws himself over her and is killed in her stead. At the end the girl dives into the vinegar jar headfirst to join the true guru, and the play ends on the grotesque tableau of her legs sticking up next to the floating head of the guru.

In *Patética* Romero has written a truly important and brilliant play on the fragility of the idealism displayed by the younger generation. Like so many young people, the two disciples are obsessed by an idealistic desire for perfection. Furthermore, this desire is hubristic to begin with, and is not held seriously, as shown by the frivolity implicit in greeting the returning guru with a shower of sunflowers; and it is helpless since the two are forever searching for a master to follow. Once their own guru is dead, they see as their only hope the appearance of the Guru of Gurus who will lead them to the elusive and illusory goal of perfection. They are thus ideal raw material for the eternal confidence game of the older generation. It is only pure coincidence that in their compulsive search for a master they fell initially under the influence of the old guru, whose asceticism, selflessness, and idealism in distributing his measures of vinegar—or harsh truth—shows him to be the true radical reformer or revolutionary. He is, further, a non-violent revolutionary since violence only leads inevitably to a single-minded conviction of rectitude, such as that shown by the Guru of Gurus. The latter, with his doctrine of refined sugar, represents the complacent right wing—a clever linking of conservative religion and commercial opportunism into one symbol. His speeches are a clever parody of the imbecilities of right-wing rhetoric:

HOLY GURU: Because [the soul] doesn't have to progress since everything is already perfect. And progress is false progress, and it is imperfection and it is regression because it is movement away from perfection . . .

PATALETA: And then what? Everything always the same, without moving?

HOLY GURU: Because there is no need to move, because there is no need to stir anything up. Because if you move a stone, a scorpion leaps out at you; if you move a boulder, the Spirit of Darkness leaps out at you.

PATALETA: But if you move the stone, you can kill the scorpion. Because the scorpion exists, the scorpion goes around alive waving its tail, under the boulder.

HOLY GURU (*accusingly*): You have been reading perverted books, books from over there: from that cursed Europe with all its diabolic countries like England, France, Australia, Germany, the United States, Russia, and Portugal, and Greece, and South Africa, and Spain, and there is no susceptibility there, no there isn't, the Archangel of the Holy Susceptibility has been killed by false progress in search of an illusory perfection. True progress is not progressing but regressing.

PATALETA: Progressing backwards?

HOLY GURU: That's it—progressing backwards, regressing.

PATALETA: Regressing where?

HOLY GURU: To perfection. Regressing, regressing, regressing . . .

PATALETA: To what perfection?

HOLY GURU: To the original perfection.

This kind of talk together with the Holy Guru's obvious cynicism in trying to seduce her, in the guise of the pursuit of the holy ideal, is too much for the girl, who throws herself into the jar as a gesture of hopelessness and lost faith. The male disciple is the type who will follow any leader who presents himself, the natural sheep who will perform philosophical pendulum swings without ever noticing it.

Pontifical is a far more difficult and complex play than *Patética*. It is, to begin with, unwieldy in length, running to 442 pages in typescript. It would, consequently, be futile to attempt a detailed description and analysis of the play since its complexity would make the commentary almost as long as the play itself.

Romero's central or core theme in *Pontifical* is the relationship between the dominating and the dominated elements in human society. As Romero sees it, the basic fact of society is that it is a structure arbitrarily built on a hierarchical principle that is unrelated to merit, ability, or justice, but is determined solely on the basis of power. This power is self-perpetuating, being either passed down from generation to generation or, more rarely, being seized by the dominated, who then become institutionalized and absorbed into the power structure. Romero's point of view approximates Genet's in *The Balcony* and Weiss's in *Marat/Sade*. All three authors reveal the paradox of the simultaneous uselessness and necessity of revolution: the dominators must be fought, even though they always remain, return, or are replaced by other dominators.

Romero's play is set in a zoo, which is a microcosm of society, of the world, or of any particular country. The power structure that runs the zoo consists of an invisible Board of Trustees—the Society for the Protection of Wild Animals—and a visible managerial team consisting of the Director, the Secretary, the Undersecretary, and the Veterinarian. Of these the most important are the Director, who represents the technocrat of the modern state, the apparent boss who is really only an intermediary between the dominators and the dominated and serves as the scapegoat responsible for his masters' decisions; and the Undersecretary, a fanatic who represents the ultraconservative position—the sort of person who does not seem to be aware that the French Revolution ever took place and who remains a willing and enthusiastic slave to an antiquated and perverse ideal. Below the administrators of the zoo are the sweepers, whose job it is to clean out the cages. They, too, are divided into various factions, most important of which are the young workers who are just starting out, who represent the radical left and who wish to stop being dominated *now*; the trade unionists, represented by the aptly named One-Eyed Man, who have become absorbed into the system and want radical change as little as the administrators do; and the quiescent masses, who break out into rebellion like rabid sheep, much in the way the lunatics in Sade's asylum do. The binder that holds these opposing factions together is self-interest, represented by the zoo's collection of wild animals, the economic resources of the society. The problem facing the zoösociety is whether to get more wild animals, i.e., develop socially and economically, or whether to carry on with the feeble and desiccated specimens they now have, i.e., remain in reactionary torpor. Some cages no longer even have animals, but only the skeletons of deceased animals. These skeletons are religiously guarded and perform an ambiguous function in the plot, since they might refer to the senile, nearly dead reactionary bureaucrats and their stubborn cult of the past, as well as to the moribund state of the society as a whole.

These various strands of meaning and allusion are brought together in an enormously intricate, ribald, and irreverent plot. This concerns a domestic crisis in the zoösociety. It seems the workers have been getting restless, feeling that even so lowly an occupation as sweeping the animals' dung out of their cages is worth a wage that provides a modicum of the comfort that the administrators ostentatiously wallow in. To make the situation worse, the workers' demands come at a most inopportune moment, since receipts have been falling as a result of lack of public interest in the zoo. Fewer and fewer people are buying tickets to see the piles of bones and the toothless and enfeebled beasts in the cages. The only exhibit that still pulls in any money is the zoo's most illustrious animal, the elephant, but he, too, is getting old and will have to be replaced. The zoo clearly cannot afford to buy another elephant, so it is decided to rent a female for breeding purposes. This presents further problems since even elephant rental is beyond the zoo's current means. The administrators feel that the rickety old buildings near the elephant house need to be shored up because the vibrations caused by the violence of the elephantine coupling might make them collapse. After much deliberation, the administrators decide that the only possible solution is to lower the salaries of the sweepers still further.

But now a new problem arises to harry the administrators. It seems that despite the elephant's great age he has never before been at stud. He is, indeed, virginal, having never been in the same cage with another elephant, and it is feared that he will not know what to do at the critical moment. After examining the beast thoroughly, the Veterinarian decides that the elephant cannot function sexually unless he is circumcised; and, hatchet in hand, he crawls underneath the elephant to operate.

The hapless elephant's martyrdom had already begun earlier, when the apprentice sweepers (the new generation of workers) persuaded the others to rebel and build a new zoo based on equal distribution of its land. The only way to do this, they felt, was to kill all the animals, beginning with the elephant. The method they selected (after discussing such others as putting hyena pups up his rear end so that they will eat their way to his heart) was defenestration. All the action involving the elephant is, of course, offstage; but the scene loses none of its hilarity by being reported. The defenestration was unsuccessful since the elephant got stuck halfway through the window with his hind end wavering in space. In any case, the rebellion was aborted by the appearance of an ecclesiastical commission, come to bless the elephant on his approaching fatherhood. It is at this point that the Veterinarian decides to circumcise the elephant, but, since he is both myopic and incompetent, he cuts the animal's trunk off instead of his prepuce. Thus the zoo's chief attraction bleeds to death before the horrified eyes of his owners. With the death of the elephant the power of the administrators is broken and a true revolution, reminiscent of the frenzy at the end of Weiss's *Marat/Sade* takes place. While the *Internationale* and the *Dies irae* are sung in counterpoint, the members of the Administration are defenestrated. The setback is purely temporary, however. As always, the oppressed do not have the power to control revolution, and the dominators return, as fresh and pristine as ever, to resume their power where they left off. At the end the reactionary Undersecretary cracks his whip over the sweepers as he howls the Administration's new official slogan: "Human relations!"

This brief description cannot begin to give an idea of the richness of the text nor of the style, much of which is a parody of Biblical cadences. It does, however, give some idea of the essence of Romero's thought. Romero sees society as divided into masters and servants, and he sees no hope for change, for the masters always return in one form or another. It should be emphasized that Romero is not writing about class struggle. The vision of society divided into the classes that historical determinists are so fond of is an implicitly optimistic view, since it believes that the positions of the classes in relation to each other have only to be reversed for social conditions to be ameliorated, if not, indeed, perfected. For Romero there are the dominators and the dominated, and membership in either category is largely fortuitous, the reason for it being the essentially psychological one of instinctive self-aggrandizement. Combined with this belief is the one Romero emphasized in *Patética*: that human beings seem to have a basic urge not to be free. Like the disciples in *Patética*, various characters in *Pontifical* look to a higher authority for orders, or seek another set of slogans to guide them. Everyone wants to be manipulated by someone else, and even the highest manipulators are subjugated to someone. Perhaps the Society for the Protection of Wild Animals is the Supreme Authority, but they too are subject, perhaps to something else such as a desiccated set of rules the reasons for which everyone has long forgotten.

Romero's strength as a playwright lies in his completely original style, in his amazing inventiveness, and in his ability to blend a series of satiric themes into a single plot. Both stylistically and philosophically he has affinities with Genet, Ghelderode, and Weiss, though the differences, as I have pointed out, are sufficient for him to be distinctly his own man.

NOTE

1. Romero has recently written a third play, *Paraphernalia de la olla podrida, la misericordia y la mucho consolación* ("Paraphernalia of the Stew, the Compassion and the Great Consolation."). All three plays are being translated into German and will be published by Suhrkamp.

8

MANUEL MARTÍNEZ MEDIERO

Manuel Martínez Mediero is one of the few authors of the new Spanish drama who has not gravitated toward Madrid or Barcelona. He continues to live in his home town of Badajoz, the chief city of Extremadura, near the Portuguese border. Like so many of his compatriots, Mediero has been awarded several prizes for playwriting. In 1969 he won the National University Prize and the Sitges Prize. The latter was awarded for *El último gallinero* ("The Last Chicken Coop,") and was produced by the Akelarre Theatre of Bilbao under the direction of Luis Iturri.

El último gallinero is clearly Mediero's most mature and important play. Like Ruibal and Romero, Mediero uses animal symbolism in this play, the run-down chicken coop serving as a microcosm of society. All the elements of modern political structure are parodied in this play. The hen house is ruled by Hermógenes, the dictator or political boss of the society, aided by his bailiff, who represents the police or army power, and keeps "order" with his truncheon. The forms and trappings of a free society are maintained in the chicken coop: when a problem affecting the welfare of the community comes up, it is put to a vote. When, however, the younger chickens who represent the rebellious New Left refuse to vote, they are beaten into submission by the bailiff while Hermógenes complacently remarks that, "this is democracy." But Hermógenes, like so many pseudo-democratic political bosses, has a weakness: the slavery that he imposes on those weaker than himself is endemic in his own character. The real rulers of the roost are the pheasant and his attendant sycophant, the turkey. These two do nothing but strut around preening themselves on their supposedly superior blood lines, hoarding their money while they live parasitically off the worker chickens and muttering resentfully about the good old days when they did not have to pretend equality. They are constantly deferred to by Hermógenes, much in the manner in which the desiccated remnants of titled heredity or the possessors of unearned wealth are deferred to in the world's nominal democracies. Throughout the play shots and other sounds of violence are heard coming from the world outside the chicken coop similar to the way the same sounds make a sinister obbligato to the action in Genet's *The Balcony*. The meaning of the violence is revealed when the inhabitants of the coop become aware of the first of two critical problems that they must face. They have been isolated by this inexplicable violence. Their normal routine has been disrupted by forces beyond their comprehension. The door, usually opened every morning to let them out into the farmyard and to admit their food, remains closed. It even seems to have been wedged shut by some men, who are also apparently bulldozing the ground around the coop and transporting chickens around in trucks. Food is running low, and the coop is basing all its hopes on a ram, the paramour of one of its capons, who has been sent for and appealed to to batter the door down. Despite their repugnance at this arrangement, the authorities and the bourgeois chickens who support them agree to it since social morality always takes second place to necessity.

Before any relief comes, however, the coop is faced with another vexing problem. The door opens momentarily and a sack is thrust in. In the sack is a wounded white cock—all the chickens in the coop are varicolored—who has been thrown out of his own coop for subversion. He informs the chickens in the "último gallinero," who seem to be totally unaware of what is going on in the world outside, that his rebellion was against the suppression of all differences and all individuality in the other chicken coops. He tells them that they are "the last chicken coop," that all the others have been converted into super-productive technocratic efficiency machines, where the chickens live in gleaming, precisely measured cages with regulated temperature and lights burning day and night. The picture he paints is very much like the inhuman society in Aldous Huxley's *Brave New World*, and he appeals to his new companions to unite in the name of universal love so that they can form a "new paradise" where all will be free and of one color. It is clear that Mediero's sympathies lie with the chaotic "last" chicken coop, since it, at least, contains the possibility of freedom and improvement that is altogether barred by the machine-like impersonality of the technocratic dictatorship in which the rest of the world is being submerged. Mediero is, however, a realist, and realists nowadays tend to be pessimists. His concern in the play is, that a society that contains the possibility of freedom and improvement will not improve and will not opt for freedom. Furthermore, even if a movement such as that of Castelar, the white cock, and his supporters among the younger generation of the varicolored chickens, were successful, it would be useless because that kind of society is already as *passé* as the one it would replace. The faceless technocratic society has all the power in its hands and it cannot be resisted. Castelar's rebellion comes to naught when the old guard captures him and stuffs him with the coop's small remaining food supply with a view to fattening him up and eating him. But although they kill Castelar, they never get a chance to eat him because at the end all the inmates of the coop are exterminated by the outside forces, who have decided that they have permitted the coop to exist long enough and simply sweep it aside.

El último gallinero is a commentary on the hopelessness of attempting to live according to traditional forms in the face of a technocratic progress gone wild—that is to say, in the face of a technocratic progress so drunk with the vista of seemingly infinite possibilities stretching out before it, that it has gone into a berserk frenzy of self-development that can only end in the destruction of everything it cannot absorb. At the same time that Mediero sees the hopelessness of the traditional forms of social life he continues to satirize them, and *El último gallinero* is a worthy addition to those social satires in the form of animal allegory such as Anatole France's *Penguin Island* and George Orwell's *Animal Farm*. The picture of the ruling society dominated by Hermógenes and the "aristocratic" pheasant and turkey is, indeed, very much like the society whose origins France described in *Penguin Island*:

"Do you see, my son," he exclaimed, "That madman who with his teeth is biting the nose of the adversary he has overthrown and that other one who is pounding a woman's head with a huge stone?"

"I see them," said Balloch, "They are creating law; they are founding property; they are establishing the principles of civilization, the
basis of society, and the foundations of the State."[1]

Mediero's sympathies are with those who have inadvertently
contributed to the founding of law, property, and civilization by
serving as victims for the strong to exercise their spurious authority
on. His concern for the underdog in society has given rise to two
plays. *Jacinta se marchó a la guerra* ("Jacinta Went to War," 1967)
is a superbly realized psychological study, sad and comic at the
same time, of the humiliating yet cunning subterfuges a penniless
old woman has to go through in order to survive in freedom. At
one point, her friends become tired of her tricks and importunities
and succeed in having her put away in an old people's home, but
Jacinta, unable to endure the impersonality, inhumanity, and the
lack of freedom, manages to escape and returns to plague her
friends once more. Slight though the apparent subject of the play
is, Mediero turns it into a moving statement about self-respect and
individuality by the acuteness of his observation and the depth of
his psychological understanding. *El convidado* ("The Guest," 1970)
is a brief one-act play that treats the same theme as *Jacinta* explores,
but this time in a symbolic rather than a realistic manner. The
characters are a father, his son, and a guest the son has invited to
dinner. The guest, who is unknown to the father, was a childhood
playmate of the son's. He is an amiable young man who remains
dumb throughout the play. The father takes an instinctive aversion
to the guest and proceeds to assault him with ever greater violence,
although he is given no provocation at all. The guest accepts these
attacks without the slightest sign of resentment. His childhood
playmate rapidly turns on him and helps the father in his various
attempts to destroy him. After several abortive tries the guest is
finally killed by being fed a roll stuck through with needles. As he
dies the father says, "It was all ridiculous. Nobody invited him to
eat with us." And the curtain falls to the sound of Handel's Hal-
lelujah Chorus. The saintlike guest, who turns the other cheek to
the end, is the mythic Scapegoat figure. The father, who is described
as circumspect, correctly dressed, and anxious, unleashes all the
pent-up resentment that he has suppressed in obedience to the
arbitrary and psychologically unrealistic rules he unquestioningly
follows. But a free spirit like the guest, who is naturally good and

94

naturally himself, is so far from the false ideal that man-in-society has set up for himself, that he brings out all the latent savagery seething just below the surface in an artificial man like the father. The fact that the father does not know his own son's childhood playmate and the fact that the son quickly forgets his affection for him and turns as savage as the father may be an indication that the guest functions also as a symbol of the lost innocence of childhood.

Mediero's other plays do not come up to the standard of those already discussed, though their defects result from over-ambitiousness rather than from inability. The most interesting of his other plays is *El hombre que fué a todas las guerras* ("The Man Who Went to All the Wars").[2]

Most of the new Spanish authors have learned to look on the endemic violence of the twentieth century with considerable cynicism, and Mediero is no exception. The protagonist of *El hombre que fué a todas las guerras* is Nicolas, a mercernary who is always hoping for a war to break out somewhere. Nicolas is a perfectly ordinary, even amiable, fellow in all other respects. His only peculiarity is that he feels unfulfilled unless he has a machine gun in his hands. The play is a panoramic view of mid-twentieth century wars and "police actions," in all of which Nicolas happily takes part. Mediero is, I think, presenting Nicolas as a dramatic symbol of the basic human impulse to senseless violence and the transformation of this impulse into a routine activity accepted as part of respectable, even "honorable," social behavior. To Nicolas mass murder is a game, an activity sanctioned by the blessing of public morality. It is a means of earning money and of self-aggrandizement. The self-respect of men like Nicolas is actually increased by playing the war game, and their actions differ only in degree and not at all in kind from those of the commanders who plan the wars. Mediero's creation of the little professional soldier, Nicolas, forces us to think of those who make his thrills possible: of generals playing with little lead soldiers in a tiny five-sided room at the core of the Pentagon; of admirals conducting war games with toy battleships and aircraft carriers in their bathtubs; of air force marshals grown too portly for the bucket seats of atomic bombers, revelling in visions of mushroom clouds and defoliated landscapes as they buzz toy airplanes round their plush offices. And below— far, far below them—the little men like Nicolas who make their dreams possible: the pathological sadomasochists, to give them their clinical name, or "soldiers of fortune," to give them their romantic one, who see war as fun and join up in Foreign Legions and private colonialist mercenary armies when nothing better offers, Jack the Rippers with the globe as their dark alley and tinsel medals or rainbow-hued combat ribbons as their reward instead of the hangman's noose.

Mediero is a playwright whose full development is still ahead of him and whose strength lies in his closeness to folk tradition and to the earthy humor and native dialect of the Spanish peasantry.

NOTES

1. Anatole France, *Penguin Island* (New York: Modern Library, 1933), pp. 44–45.

2. Mediero has also written *Espectáculo del siglo XX* ("Twentieth Century Show,"), *Adolf*, *Las planchadoras* ("The Ironing Women," 1971), and *El regreso de los escorpiones* ("The Return of the Scorpions," 1971).

9

LUIS MATILLA

Luis Matilla was born in San Sebastián during the last months of the Spanish Civil War. He is thus a member of the younger generation of the new Spanish dramatists, those whose minds were formed during the oppression and austerities of the immediate post-war period. The acuteness of perception, the extensive questioning of values, and the sensitivity to current philosophical ideas in other countries of men like Matilla, López Mozo, and García Pintado is especially remarkable in view of their growing up in a period when Spain was almost completely isolated from the rest of the world. At this time, too, the educational system was rigidly supervised by the authorities for the purpose of instilling single-minded patriotism and re-writing history in accordance with the new order, as happens in other modern dictatorships. The thinking of these men and many of their compatriots is as original and perceptive as the thinking of their contemporaries in countries like France, England, and the United States, where there have been no obstacles to the free exercise of intellectual curiosity. Indeed, the obstacles may have had the peculiar effect of clarifying the thinking of the Spanish dramatists. The Spaniard, constantly faced with obstructions to free expression, living in a society where the inequalities are so blatant and where the hierarchical structure is so clearly defined, can identify the problem. Where the young writer in a free country tends to vacillate, shifting from one point of view to another, unable to find a constant direction for his thought and work, the young

Spanish writer has no doubts—*can* have no doubts. The basic problems of the artist—freedom of expression and the burden laid on men by the errors of history—confront him constantly. To the young Spaniard, as to so many members of the younger generation throughout the Western world, the errors of history are summed up and encapsulated in the immediately preceding generation. The powerlessness of the older generation to cope morally with the technological progress they have achieved appears as the central fact of life to the younger generation. They feel themselves less the inheritors of a tradition that they must advance as it has been advanced serially before them by preceding generations than the initiators of a new way the necessity of which has been forced on them by the definitive failure of the old. Sometimes this feeling is expressed in hope, sometimes in pugnacious assertion, as in López Mozo's *The Testament*, where the grandson contemptuously destroys the will in which his grandparents have tried to justify their actions, or as in Matilla's *El monumento erecto*, where the younger generation blows up the monument symbolizing the older generation's achievements; sometimes it is expressed in despair, as in Matilla's *Post-Mortem*, where the young people are surrounded and entrapped wherever they go, or as in his *Una guerra en cada esquina* ("A War in Every Corner," 1968), where the young rebels are helpless against the entrenched forces and are finally destroyed with them. Alberto Miralles, the Barcelona-based playwright and critic, has described the attitude that pervades the theater of the younger playwrights succinctly by quoting Albert Szent-Györgyi, Nobel Prize winner for medicine in 1937, "I have already given up writing for adults; they cannot be convinced. The only thing that can be done for them is to give them time to die." He follows this up with a quote from John Lindsay: "The most important task facing youth today is that of pointing out and unmasking those institutions that have not done what it was their responsibility to do, such as governments that do nothing to fight hunger."[1] Miralles is asserting the principal theme of the younger generation, to wit, the failure of the older generation; and he has chosen his quotations to describe the two principal attitudes to the theme: total contemptuous rejection, and a determination to fight for a better world coupled with an excoriation of those who have made the fight necessary.

All Luis Matilla's plays are concerned either with this conflict between the generations, or with the attrition of personal or artistic dignity through the oppressiveness of political systems whose paranoia and mindlessness have led them to value efficiency more than humanity. There has, of course, always been generational conflict. As a result of it mankind has made its tortuous, crabwise advance as each generation rebelled mildly, achieved some slight improvement in the body social and politic, and then quietly succumbed into the role of the older generation in its turn as its members began imperceptibly to dissolve into their component chemical elements. The conflict depicted in the plays of Matilla and the other young Spanish dramatists is, however, a radical one. This is not a matter of re-arrangement for purposes of amelioration: it is a matter of replacement. The older generation has brought the social situation to the point of irreversible putrescence, and the only solution is an entirely new growth.

Matilla sharply points up this view by repeatedly using death as his symbol for the older generation. In *Post-Mortem* (1970) death and the older generation triumph; in *El monumento erecto* ("The Standing Monument") they are defeated. In both cases, though, the equation of death with the traditional way of life is a masterstroke of dramatic symbolism.

In *El monumento erecto*[2] the scene is a bare room with a peculiar looking pyramidal monument in the middle. On closer inspection this monument turns out to be a war memorial consisting of the helmeted skulls of those fallen in the most recent of the "great" wars (as distinct from the frequent "little" wars instigated to give the economy a temporary boost). The two chief characters are an old woman, whose job it is to climb all over the monument pouring lime into the cracks so that it will not collapse, and a young woman who is looking for her dead husband's remains so that she can collect his pension, since it is the rule that survivors must produce some part of the victim's body to qualify. Because this play is about the perversion of love in the mind of a person who unthinkingly accepts a society that will proudly erect monuments to "glorious" death, Matilla cynically juxtaposes the young woman's mercenary intentions with the words of conventional romantic "love" which she speaks, quite unconscious of any incongruity, to what she believes are her husband's remains. Not everyone looks on the monument with the imbecilic devotion of the young war widow, however. Her obsequies are interrupted by a bill poster who puts up an election placard ironically touting a peace candidate, and by a man who does not have such a high opinion of war as the rest of society (and is, therefore, considered mad) and urinates on the monument. A young man comes in and makes elaborate preparations for dynamiting the monument. The curator attempts to dissuade him by appealing to all the conventional sentiments. The young man does not even deign to look at him, but, after completing his arrangements, he attacks the curator. His face completely impassive, he beats the curator "as if his hatred had been contained for centuries." The impassiveness indicates that he is punishing rather than fighting. Nevertheless, in doing so the young man has left his task and has become involved with the older generation, if ever so remotely and impersonally. He has, therefore, in a sense, sold out and become unworthy of his task. Becoming involved is the first step toward joining, and so, while the curator is being beaten, an eight year old child comes in and detonates the explosion, leaving only himself alive.

This is as absolute a piece of social nihilism as we are likely to find in modern writing. The association of the older generation with the obscene monument in which it preens itself on its success in negating life, and the assertion that hope lies only in the destruction of the old order by those who have remained entirely uncontaminated by it combines hope and despair in a uniquely ambiguous synthesis. *El monumento erecto* is a play that can be understood either as an expression of faith in a future controlled by a new generation, or as a statement of cynical, mocking despair.

In *Post-Mortem* there is no ambiguity. The old order triumphs— not with the clear finality of an explosion, but with a more realistic encirclement and slow asphyxiation of the rebellious instincts of the younger generation. Once again Matilla uses death as a symbol of the established order. The inspiration for the play came from Jessica Mitford's exposé of the undertaking business in *The American Way of Death*, which demonstrated that the success of that most superfluous of all businesses was based on society's worship of death. By using a funeral parlor as the principal setting of his play Matilla simultaneously symbolizes the lifelessness of established society and its elevation of death to the level of an ideal. He realistically depicts the hypocrisy of the society in the contrast between the deliberately deceptive façade of the reception rooms, pervaded with incense and music, and the hidden truth of the embalming rooms, where dead bodies are pumped up, made-up, resected, and clamped together again.

The play opens in a funeral parlor where a young man whose father has just died and a girl who has just lost her mother are waiting in adjoining rooms, one decorated like the chapel of a castle, the other like a Russian monastery. The establishment is the type that drums up business by having its agents hide under the beds of the recently deceased with advertising circulars and contracts, ready to crawl forth and sign up the survivors. Matilla's animadversion to the pursuit of profit, single-minded to the point of callousness, of the established business world is clear enough and typical of his sardonic wit. Death is always referred to in this business as *el hecho* ("the fact") and coffins as places of repose. The young man instinctively rebels at the hypocrisy implicit in this careful obscurantism, but the girl tries to calm him and counsels him to obey the time-honored customs. Matilla carefully has the girl's advice, as well as the admonitions of the unctuous and sinister undertaker—the only other character in the play—sound as if the young man's objections to the fee gouging and tastelessness of the funeral home are really much more serious than would appear—as if his rejection of funerary shibboleths were a socially subversive act or a defiance of the law. The undertaking establishment, in other words, represents a repressive society in which traditions are followed for their own sake and in which subservience to them is required precisely because they make no sense. The girl is won over to the cause of rebellion when the young man shows her the preparation room, where she sees her mother's body with the hands cut off and wax ones substituted to make the corpse look prettier for the lying in state. The undertaker advises her not to take this glimpse of reality too seriously: "Try not to think—it's the only way to achieve complete peace of mind." The two young people, however, steal their parents' bodies and drag the coffins away intending to find a plot of free ground in which to bury them. But the undertaker keeps popping up in their way no matter how far they go:

YOUNG MAN: We're looking for some free ground.
MAN (*as if searching his memory*): Free ground . . . free ground. (*Pause. Decisively.*) No, there's no free ground here, and I don't believe there's any further away either.

No matter where they go, the land seems to have been bought up by the undertakers, who are taking over the country in the name of progress—and death. "It is possible that in a very short time we will have succeeded in converting the whole country into one huge cemetery," the undertaker informs them proudly and with totally unconscious irony. Matilla brings his play to its climax at this point as he makes his mordant equation between progress (i.e., technology) and death. Technological progress plus mindless obedience to calcified traditions equals dehumanization equals death. The play ends with the defeat of the two freedom seekers; the undertakers already own all the earth.

Post-Mortem is a play that ends in despair. *Funeral* (1968) is a commentary on that despair. Once again the theme is death as a symbol of the lifelessness of society, but this time Matilla gives us an ironic comment on the pervasive worship of death-in-life. The scene is again a room in a funeral parlor, where a flag-draped coffin is awaiting burial. The coffin supposedly holds what remains of a young man who has been killed in the war. Three men dressed in mourning enter during the course of the play. One is in his sixties, one is in his forties, and one is in his twenties. All of them are professional funeral orators. Apparently all but one of them have lost their way since each one is under the impression that he has been hired to pronounce the funeral oration over this particular corpse. While waiting to find out who is right and getting more and more drunk, they discuss their contrasting philosophies on heroic funeral orations. The older generation talks about its heroes with flowery lyricism and prates about the glory of death, while the middle generation—the one now in power—preens itself on talking about the realism of war and inspiring the survivors to sacrifice themselves: "Our generation has learned how to justify death; yours only tried to make it poetic. You fooled men into sacrificing themselves; we want to show them the horror and the cruelty so that their efforts may have a real value." The youngest orator shocks both of the older ones by having prepared a speech that deals specifically with the particular dead hero he has been assigned. This concern with the individual is profoundly disturbing to the two older men, who, each in his own way, have been concerned only with generalities, with men in the mass, manipulating them for their own purposes. To the older generations the dead man serves only as a tool for levering more men like him toward death. They are propagandists rather than mourners, caring nothing for the men whose actions and sacrifice they describe so grandiloquently and insincerely. The youngest generation does care, but Matilla ends his play with ironic cynicism as all three orators become totally drunk and dissolve in helpless laughter as they contemplate their predicament.

In *El monumento erecto, Post-Mortem,* and *Funeral* Matilla writes about the generational conflict using death as his image of the old order. The constant theme running through all his plays, however, is the sacredness and supremacy of the individual, and his struggle to maintain his identity. Death is the ultimate rejection and the appropriate symbol for a generation approaching its extinction and jealous of the life that will remain when it is gone. Matilla treats the theme humorously in *Juegos de amanecer* ("Dawn Games," 1969). In the pre-dawn darkness of an apartment meticulously decorated in the latest style two apparently young people try very hard to convince themselves that they are in the swing of things, playing rock music, constantly asking each other if their clothes and make-up are in the right style, reassuring each other that they are playing the right music and dancing the right dances. They feel that now at last they will be free and will not be laughed at. At the end the energy of their dancing makes their heavy make-up run and their wigs fall askew, revealing them as a pitifully old couple. The dawn enters the musty apartment bringing the light and life they can no longer even imitate. There is something enormously pathetic and compassionate in this portrayal of an older generation lost in a world that has passed them by and has been taken over and transformed by a new order that they try sedulously to imitate.

Matilla displays a curiously ambiguous and indecisive attitude in his generational plays, sometimes showing despair, sometimes fantasy, and sometimes compassion. It is the ambiguity of the true artist and thinker, however—the doubt of the man who perceives problems and sets questions. Art that provides answers is totalitarian art.

In his other principal plays Matilla deals with more specific encroachments on freedom. In *El piano* ("The Piano," 1970) he investigates the degradation of the artist in a totalitarian society, summing it up in the dramatic image of a pianist who is scheduled to perform a concerto for piano and orchestra, without an orchestra. Kos, the pianist, lives in a society in which his art is unwanted. He is, in fact, the last musician left in the country. Audiences prefer music played by machines. His piano is the only musical instrument of any kind left in this land of technology-worshipping Philistines, and his discouragement is so profound that he hardly plays it anymore. When he does play, he plays only dissonances, but most of the time he sleeps in it, makes coffee in it, keeps his books and his birdcage in it, and laments the disappearance of the orchestras he used to perform with. He has a concert scheduled, but only four people, one of them deaf, show up for it. Even this last gasp of the country's artistry is stifled when a government official comes to forbid the performance and seals the piano. Kos is taken away at the end by his wife and a friend, completely defeated by the society from which all other artists have been driven and in which he can no longer function. His delirious plan to drag the piano away bodily into the mountains and play there in the free air sums up the artist's impractical but unconquerable determination to continue despite all obstacles, and the dramatic image of the pianist without accompaniment or audience sums up the plight of the artist in a country that misprizes his art and prevents the exercise of it.

A society that deprecates art also tends toward prurience and invasion of privacy. Totalitarian societies have always leaned strongly toward Puritanism through an association of sexual freedom (i.e., freedom in its most personal form) and public freedom. Similarly, they have invariably had an active prejudice against individual privacy as a result of their exaltation of the public weal (i.e., the good of the State as arbitrarily defined by those in power) over private life.

Matilla treats these two themes in *La ventana* ("The Window," 1967) and *El observador* ("The Observer," 1969), both one-act plays in which he continues his trenchant examination of society today. *La ventana*, the weaker of the two plays, concerns sexual hypocrisy and prurience. Two passers-by see the silhouette of two women kissing on a window screen. They bring some other people to see the scene the next evening and denounce the two women to the police. When they are led away, the two women are seen to be old and in despair at losing each other's companionship. The main point of the play is the revelation of the hang-ups and socially induced frustrations of the Peeping Toms as they wait for the scene to be repeated. Matilla shows us that sexual prurience is an activity limited to minds that have been so repressed and steam-rollered into unquestioning conformity to senseless rules of behavior that they can think of nothing better to do than pry into the lives of people they suspect of a deficiency in conformity.

El observador is one of Matilla's best plays, on a level with *Post-Mortem and El monumento erecto.* It is also, unfortunately, his most topical play. *El observador* is a satire on official interference with privacy—the sort of interference which wiretapping, eavesdropping, mail censorship, and sleek, polite men questioning neighbors and fellow-workers have made familiar to people all over the world in recent years. The "observer" in Matilla's play is one of those sleek, gray men who have become so ubiquitous. He is assigned to "observe" a man who has been guilty of some vague excess of free thought. To "observe" in this sense means to be with him always, and in the play we see the "observer," who never speaks, calmly pulling up a chair to watch the man and his wife prepare for bed. Matilla achieves a chillingly sinister effect as the wife awkwardly attempts to undress under the sheets, while his impassive gaze is unwaveringly fixed on her. The force of the effect comes, of course, from our premonitory indentification with the situation. The only place the man can think anymore is the lavatory, but when he goes there this time the "observer" follows him, locks him in, and then returns, impassive as ever, and pulls the sheet off the woman as the lights go out. In this play Matilla, even more than in his "death" plays, has succeeded in creating a dramatic situation that brings together a social problem which is becoming more and more pressing and a psychological fear that lies ever closer to the surface of consciousness in all human beings that still aspire to be individuals.

Luis Matilla's plays are the most mature ones produced by the authors of the younger generation of the underground movement. His contemporaries, while showing unmistakable signs of developing mastery, are still groping for a style and an attitude that will express their inner being, but Matilla has already found them. He is a fully mature writer, and *Post-Mortem, El monumento erecto,* and *El observador,* at least, will certainly take their recognized place in the modern Spanish drama.

NOTES

1. Alberto Miralles, "Teatro 1970: Una generación sin oportunidades," *Mundo*, September 5, 1970, p. 26.

2. This play, together with *Juegos de amanecer* and *Semillas de romboendros*, is in a collection entitled *Ejercicios para amantes* ("Exercises for Lovers").

10

ANGEL GARCÍA PINTADO AND DIEGO SALVADOR

With regard to the playwrights treated so far, the Spanish underground drama movement is virtually a saga of triumph in the face of adversity. The censors have not been able to prevent the growth of a distinctive dramatic movement consisting of an appreciable number of plays of high literary quality. Despite the assiduity of their vigilant pettiness, despite their total incomprehension of literary values, despite their politically pragmatic arbitrariness, a countermovement has managed to flourish in the contemporary Spanish theater that will inevitably survive and eclipse the ephemeral plays that have passed their scrutiny. Though rarely published and rarely produced, the plays of a Castro, a Ruibal, a Bellido, or a Ballesteros are, nonetheless, able to win out, and to be recognized by the Spanish cultural and academic community as the drama that represents the continuity of the Spanish dramatic tradition. This is not to say, of course, that the censorship has not had a deleterious effect. With the exception of Buero-Vallejo, who has had fairly consistent success in having his plays produced, all these authors have suffered to some extent by their inability to learn from the experience of seeing their works under performance conditions. They have, nevertheless, continued writing with a dogged persistence that once more seems to prove that genius is the infinite capacity for taking pains.

107

The story of the Spanish underground drama is not, unhappily, a continuous saga of triumphant artistry versus thwarted officialdom. Inevitably the lack of opportunity to obtain practical experience and the discouragement that goes with that lack has taken its toll. Writers such as Angel García Pintado and Diego Salvador are men of obvious theatrical talent and creativity whose plays have been seriously flawed by the restrictions under which they are forced to work. Their plays show clear promise and are shot through with flashes of theatrical ability of a high order, but they lack the cohesiveness of structure that alone could bind their ideas into a theatrical whole. The blame for this must be placed squarely on the censorship, for these men are clearly, on the basis of the work that they have done so far, potentially outstanding playwrights. The deeper effect that the censorship seems to have had on them than on their contemporaries such as Matilla, Mediero, and López Mozo can be explained only partially by a difference in degree of talent: the true explanation is basically a psychological one.

Both Pintado and Salvador are among the theoretical leaders of the younger wing of the movement. The problems facing them and the Spanish theatre in general are perfectly clear to them and they have spoken out cogently on the subject. Perhaps, indeed, part of the psychological factor that has inhibited them to some extent in the writing of their plays lies in their perception of the problem and in their preoccupation with the theoretical analysis of the situation. The degree to which an author is hampered in his work by the knowledge that it will have to be submitted to a censor whose primary concern will not be its literary value varies considerably, of course, from one individual to another; and Pintado and Salvador are examples of authors who have been intensely affected by their situation.

Pintado has been able to see his own problem as clearly as anyone. He has stated publicly that the lack of theatrical laboratories has caused substantial injury to the evolution of the contemporary Spanish drama and he has criticized the independent (i.e., noncommercial) theater groups in Spain for not doing enough to support the new playwrights, accusing them of having too much fear and not enough faith.[1] This is perhaps a little too harsh. The inability of the independent and university theater groups to help the development of the new Spanish drama is almost certainly due less to fear and lack of faith than to the unfortunate and silly rivalries between the various groups, which lead to the indiscriminate condemnation of anything done by any other group, as López Mozo has pointed out.[2] This fact is, indeed, obvious to anyone who has witnessed the disgraceful cat-calling and foot-stamping that so often mars independent theater productions in Spain.

Angel García Pintado was born in Valladolid and is now in his early thirties. He has lived in Madrid since he was a small child and was formerly on the staff of one of the leading Madrid newspapers. Pintado's principal topic is the moral erosion in the newly affluent Spanish society. He has characterized himself as a writer whose inspiration comes from political sources—or, more precisely, from the frustrations attendant upon being a man with a moral conscience in a society in which morality is equated with economic affluence. His two most interesting plays, *Crucifixión* (1967/68) and *Ocio-celo-pasión de Jacinto Disipado* ("Idleness-Envy-Passion of Jacinto Spendthrift," 1970), both deal with this subject.

Crucifixión is set on a curve on a deserted highway at night. The headlights of a car pick out the figure of a crucified man just off the road. The car stops and a man and woman, whom we soon recognize, in Pintado's skillful characterization, as a prototypical dull middle class couple, get out to investigate. Once they are convinced that the astounding apparition is really what it seems to be, the husband drives off to get a ladder and ropes so that they can lower the man, leaving his wife and young son to keep him company. The rest of the play consists of the crucified man's conversation with the wife and its effect on the son. The man belongs to a kind of heedless, bored, jet-set society whose only purpose in life seems to be a frenzied, self-annihilating quest for anaesthetizing distraction. Well-educated but not intelligent enough to use the knowledge they have gained, rich but too indolent to use their money constructively, these people spend their lives trying to fill the void that their lack of moral conviction has made out of their existences with perverted pleasures. The man, who is never given a name since his moral nullity cannot lift him above anonymity, has been nailed up as a joke born of boredom by his companions, and he is now deriving a perverse satisfaction from the novelty of his situation in a manner worthy of the imagination of de Sade himself. The wife is bored, but for other reasons. Just as the man before her is bored by the meaninglessness of a life without responsibility, she is bored by the strain of a life too full of prohibitions, obligations, and worries. Unconvinced by the reasons and values of the monotonous, petit-bourgeois life that her social destiny has imposed on her, she is thrilled and attracted by the apparent glamor of the man's life. She tries to make advances to him and hopes for some relationship with him when he is freed, but there is an essential and insurmountable barrier between the two classes that they represent. Only under the bizarre circumstances in which they meet can there be any communication between them. The child passes from innocence to cynicism as he watches them. And Pintado's point, too, is an essentially cynical one. A society in which there are human beings that are as shut off from each other by economic distinctions as these two are, in which approaching death is the *only* common denominator, has passed the point of no return. Pintado's play is not merely about the bizarre death of a useless human being: it is a dirge for a society on the road to suicide.

The moral concept of *Crucifixión* is overpowering and profound, but Pintado has ultimately been unsuccessful in putting that concept into theatrical terms. The problem lies in his choice of the play's central image. The image of the Crucifixion is too intense and pretentious for the theme of the moral bankruptcy of the idle rich and the frustrations born of ignoble desires shown by the middle class. As a dramatic symbol the Crucifixion has been overused in any case, but when it is used, it must, because of its universal associations in the Western world, be used to refer to martyrdom, sacrifice, and salvation. Here it does not, though Pintado may be intending an ironic cheapening of the symbol by using it as the material for a perverse jest by the idle rich. From the purely theatrical viewpoint there is a problem too, for the situation is incredible visually. The man necessarily exhibits so little indication of actually being crucified that his attempts to free himself run the risk of merely seeming comic. The play has, of course, been banned by the censors.

Ocio-celo-pasión de Jacinto Disipado, for which Pintado received the 1970 Guipúzcoa Prize, starts, like *Crucifixión*, with a magnificent conception, though this time it is a comic one. Jacinto Disipado is the consumer *par excellence*. His boast is that he owns everything. He is the advertising huckster's dream: gullibility personified. Jacinto lives for and through his gadgets. He worships the idea of technological progress, about which he understands nothing, with the same blind and confident devotion that his forebears paid to religion. The salesman's patter soothes him the way the propitiatory incantations of priests and medicine men soothe less developed beings who have not yet located their God in the machine. For the type of man whom Jacinto represents the concept of the *deus ex machina* has become literally true, but the machine is the television set or the vacuum cleaner. McLuhan has pointed out that machines are extensions of the body, but in Jacinto's case the process has become so complete that he exists only as the hub of his machines. His body has become, in effect, so atrophied that it no longer controls the machines but only reacts to their vibrations. Like the crucified man, Jacinto is a member of the wealthy upper crust, and he sublimates his boredom and feeling of emptiness in possessions. He lives in an incredibly cluttered apartment where every mechanical gadget imaginable is piled about haphazardly. He is, consequently, the prisoner of his possessions, a fact that is perhaps unnecessarily emphasized by a chain attached to his ankle. Jacinto is a true example of what Heimito von Doderer called the emblematic man, who orders his life in accordance with a set of symbols constituting a behavior pattern imposed on him from outside. The Jacinto type is to be found everywhere that affluence exists, of course. Nor is he a new phenomenon: his obsessions have merely changed direction toward the machine. Spain's previous version was based on artificial class distinctions instead of money. Gerald Brenan gives a fascinating description of such a man in *South from Granada*:

Jaime . . . was a man who had deliberately sacrificed his personality to a great ideal—that of being a perfect and finished gentleman. For the perfect gentleman, as he saw it, is a man who cannot allow himself any deviation from the norm. He must be as indistinguishable from all the other perfect gentlemen of his club as a pebble on the seashore is from the other pebbles of its beach. This meant that he was obliged to suppress whatever inclinations to self-assertion he may once have had and to pursue the narrow road of correctness in dress, conversation, opinions, manner, calligraphy, way of spending time, acquaintances and everything else.[3]

There is something very English in this description, but each country has its examples, the American version being the "Playboy" ape who is so terribly concerned that he is drinking the correct—i.e., advertised—brand of whisky and that he has the right labels sewn into his clothes. The emblematic man has to do everything by rote since his devotion to the artificial ideal on which he is modelling himself has completely dehumanized him, i.e., deprived him of his own initiative of action. Jacinto makes love to his mistress "with enthusiasm, as if it were an obligation to be fulfilled periodically" while she pretends to be in ecstasy because that is what is expected of her in that situation. The "love scene" is played out to the recital of a list of consumer goods chanted with mounting excitement. Everything that is done is done to the accompaniment of the appropriate advertising slogan (otherwise how would Jacinto know that it is good?). Pintado's satire is true and straight to the mark, but the play suffers from the lack of a plot. Nothing really happens, and the whole play is essentially a series of repetitions of the initial situation. Brilliantly conceived though that situation is, it is not enough to carry a whole play. *Crucifixión* suffers from the same flaw, as do Pintado's other plays, such as *Gioconda-Cicatriz* ("Gioconda-Scar," 1970), which is about the older generation stifling the younger one with its memories of the glories of war. The conceptions of Pintado's plays are in themselves more than sufficient proof of the reality and genuineness of his talent; the blame for their flaws must be attributed directly to the censorship, which makes it impossible for young authors of an unorthodox bent to develop their craft by observing it in practice.

Diego Salvador was born in Madrid in 1938, began work at fourteen, and is entirely self-educated. He has written six novels, none of which has been published, and thirteen plays. Of these works he now rejects all but the last three, the previous ones being considered by him as apprentice works. The last three are all plays: *La mujer y el ruido* ("The Woman and the Noise," 1967), which was a finalist in the Lope de Vega prize competition of 1968, *Los niños* ("The Children," 1967), which won the 1969 Lope de Vega competition, and *La bolsa* ("The Purse," 1969).

The early works that he now rejects were written in a realistic style, but Salvador's three latest plays are all in an abstract mode. In *La mujer y el ruido* and *La bolsa* Salvador has tried to portray the basic economic motives on which society is based by means of expressionistic technique. In *Los niños* he has written a play set in an apparently realistic milieu that is actually a symbolic representation of what Salvador conceives to be some of the basic diseases of contemporary society. In *La mujer y el ruido* and *La bolsa* he expounds his belief that man has created a vicious self-destructive circle with his concept of society. Salvador sees society as a sort of huge machine that swallows men up in its maw and spews them out again stripped of their potential individuality. The only way men can think of to assert themselves under these circumstances is, perversely, by devoting themselves heart and soul to the accumulation of riches, thus fueling the very machine that has ground them down in the first place. In *La bolsa* the young man who is the play's expressionistic protagonist clutches his purse as if it were an anchor or a talisman and constantly hears the figures of his imagination, who are the other characters of the play, tell him that "In order to be respected and looked up to by the rest, you must have an economic position that will raise your standing in society; otherwise you will be a failure." Salvador's analysis of the ills of society as being economically based is valid enough and shrewd. But here we can again see the tremendous stultifying influence of the censorship system that has prevented Salvador from seeing his plays done on stage. His analysis, as I have said, is valid and interesting, but it is not dramatic. To write a play the theme of which is man's enslavement by the economics of society is extremely risky in theatrical terms; and it is not helped by a mixture of styles. The characters in both *La bolsa* and *La mujer y el ruido* are abstract characters in an abstract setting, but they act out their emotions with an intensity that causes their depiction to pass from realism (which would itself be the wrong style for abstract characters) to melodrama. It should be emphasized here, as in the case of Pintado, that these plays remain enormously interesting intellectually; it is their theatrical viability that is in doubt.

Los niños is certainly Salvador's best play to date. It takes place on an empty stage that is supposedly being prepared before our eyes for a photographic exhibition of "our world and the realities of our century." Our world and the realities of our century being what they are, such an exhibition naturally consists of a series of horror pictures showing deprivation, cruelty, and injustice contrasted with a series of serene pictures showing human beings wallowing in comfort and luxury and ostentatiously unaware of the horror. The point of the play is made by the reactions of the various characters to these pictures, each of them being symbolic of a typical psychological attitude. The organizer and director of the exhibition sees the pictures simply as the core of a project he hopes will at last launch his career into the big-time of show business after years of struggle. The narrator who will guide customers through the exhibition sees them simply as something for him to describe in the beautiful, pear-shaped tones he has developed after years of practice. The two scene-shifters who bring the pictures in and hang them are brutally insensitive to what they see. It is merely a job to them, and they will do anything else they are ordered to. Sensitivity to the suffering of the world and shock at the heartlessness of its incongruities is incorporated in *los niños*, the three children of the title. One is dressed in yellow, one in white, and one in black to symbolize the three principal races. These children play light-heartedly at first but grow up during the play as they slowly become aware, through the successive pictures, of the reality they have been born into. Despite their struggles against it, they gradually become brutalized and succumb to the refuge of insensitivity at the end. The basis of the play is a cogent and well thought out parable. The trouble with it as a stage work is its excessively obvious use of melodrama and direct audience appeal. To juxtapose a picture of a starving child and a contented businessman is enough: the point is instantly made and need not be amplified with an elaborate theatrical structure.

Los niños won the 1969 Lope de Vega Prize—perhaps Spain's most prestigious—one of the provisions of which is a guarantee of the play's performance at the Teatro Español, the official government theater in Madrid. The manner in which the theater fulfilled its obligation to produce the Lope de Vega prizewinner in Salvador's case became something of a *cause célèbre* during the 1970 theatrical season. It was originally scheduled to be produced in January, was postponed to March, then to May, and finally announced for the 4th of June. A few hours before the curtain was to go up it was postponed again and did not finally open until June 19th, almost at the end of the season.[4] The late opening assured that the play would have a very short run and that it would play to virtually empty houses during that run, since by the latter part of June theatregoing in Madrid becomes rather uncomfortable since there is no air-conditioning, and most of the regular theater public has left town anyway. The reasons for all these postponements have to do with the photographs specified by Salvador for the exhibition. Salvador had carefully avoided any national references in his descriptions, but the theater administration or the censors felt that the United States was intended and insisted that at least one overt reference to Russia be made in the pictures of violence. Because of the changes made in his play Salvador formally withdrew from responsibility for the production and declined to profit by it, specifying that his royalties be given to a home for retired actors.

The experience of *Los niños* is a perfect example of the sort of thing that inhibits the development of young playwrights. Depending on one's susceptibility to this kind of harassment, one is inevitably more or less discouraged by the knowledge that someone else will be the final arbiter of one's work.

NOTES

1. *Mundo*, September 5, 1970, p. 36.
2. *Primer Acto*, No. 123–124 (1970), p. 74.
3. Gerald Brenan, *South from Granada* (New York: Farrar, Straus and Cudahy, 1957), p. 234.
4. *Primer Acto*, No. 121 (1970), p. 21.

11

MIGUEL RELLÁN

Miguel Angel Rellán was born in Tetuán, Morocco in 1943. He received his early education in religious schools, where, as he puts it, he underwent a course of systematic brutalization. Subsequently he studied medicine and recently received his M.D. degree. Rellán's two most important plays are *La puerta* ("The Door," 1967), produced in Seville, and *El guerrero ciego* ("The Blind Warrior," 1967), which won the Talavera Prize. Both these plays are among the very best produced by the Spanish underground drama.

La puerta is a one-act satiric play directed against the pretentiousness of the Spanish pseudo-aristocracy—the debased modern version of the *hidalgo*. Two ridiculous looking specimens of this class meet in front of a door, which they both wish to enter. Like Pintado's Jacinto Disipado, these are emblematic men, creatures whose personalities are non-existent and whose every action is governed by their subservience to an imposed ideal. They differ from Pintado's character, however, in being anachronistic throwbacks. Jacinto Disipado is the modern emblematic man who has been molded by advertising propaganda and whose character is shaped by the possessions he has accumulated. Don Porfirio and Don Domitilo are traditional emblematic men who have been molded by their belief that character is defined by family tree, titles, medals, and social position. They represent the parasitic class that lives on inherited wealth and rents, and considers work demeaning. Their thought processes are confined to the trivialities of social

116

privilege, such as who shall enter the door first. When they have determined that they are of exactly equal ancestral lineage and that they each own precisely the same number of decorations, they vie with each other in hypocritical expressions of self-abnegation, each insisting that the other must enter first. Rellán builds a brilliant and hilarious, deeply-cutting social satire out of this trivial puerility. The dispute is treated with ever growing grotesque caricature. The obvious solution of both entering together does not work because one of the pseudo-aristocrats is too fat. Finally they decide to get around this by entering simultaneously with one riding piggy-back on the other. This too ends in disaster because the fat one wins the toss entitling him to ride on top and the other one cannot manage the weight. By this time they have been joined by a militant association of females marching for chastity, all of whom tumble around together when the fat man topples off. The matter is finally settled by a duel in which the pseudo-aristocrats kill each other as well as the bewildered plebeian passer-by whom they have drummed into service as referee. Such a brief outline of the plot can give only an inadequate idea of the cogency and precision of Rellán's satire. Some indication of his attitude toward the society he depicts here can be gained from the fact that the whole street is blown up at the end through the explosion of a laboratory that is revealed to be behind the door. The hypocrisy and selfishness of the two protagonists, shown by their cavalier attitude to everything that does not suit their convenience, and their conviction that they are superior to the laws of the society on which they are burgeoning and which they pretend to lead is shown in numerous subtle touches of characterization and in the implicit contrast that Rellán makes between them and the "ordinary" working members of society. Don Porfirio and Don Domitilo are not isolated eccentric anachronisms peculiar to Spanish society. Despite the farcical caricature with which they are portrayed, they are fully realized universal characters whose creation is shot through with the author's savage irony. Their death in a ludicrous duel is a fitting end to their grotesquely misspent existences, and the final explosion is a mordant judgment on the society that tolerates them.

With *El guerrero ciego* Rellán moves from social satire to metaphysical protest. The scene is a condemned cell in which an old man is waiting to be executed. There is a clear implication that his death is unjust and that capital punishment is legalized butchery performed with the blessings of a time-serving and hypocritical Church, but this is only a subsidiary factor in the play. The central point of the play is concentrated in the figure of a medieval warrior in full armor that the condemned man has drawn on the wall of the cell. The warrior is blind because the man ran out of chalk before he could draw in his eyes. In one of several dream scenes that take up the greater part of the play the warrior comes alive and condemns the man for creating him blind in much the same way as the man condemns *his* Creator for bringing him into a world where he had to kill to survive and into which he was born only to die. The man tries to adopt the merciless and arbitrary attitude of a Supreme Being toward the warrior since he has created him and can do with him as he will, just as he imagines has been done unto him by whatever Power (he does not believe in the formal God of religion) is responsible for his plight. But the warrior refuses to accept this argument since the man is not self-created either. Those who are condemning the man to destruction are not self-created either, of course, and Rellán's point is that man cannot arrogate supreme power over his fellow creatures to himself. This is only the first level of Rellán's complex meaning, however. The condemned man's concentration on finishing his drawing of the warrior in his last hours is reminiscent of the struggle for complete consciousness and justification *to himself* of Camus' Meursault. Like Meursault, Rellán's anonymous condemned man is conscious of his own inward independence and integrity, and he rejects the spuriousness of the comforts of religion that are offered to him in much the same terms. In another one of the dream scenes the man sees himself as a creature in a limbo of his own imagination from which he is dragged by celestial guardians in order to be born. The celestial guardians, who look very much like the prison guards but with unearthly touches, act blindly and unquestioningly on orders from a Supreme Master and drag the man off to be born into the misery they describe to him as implacably as the prison guards drag him off to be killed. The scene in which this simultaneous birth and death occurs could easily have slipped into crass sentimentalism, as similar scenes have so often in the past, but it is saved by Rellán's masterful control of his situation. This scene, in which Rellán equates the moments of birth and death showing that man is forced out of his life as he was forced into it by powers beyond his comprehension and control, is theater of cruelty in the pure sense intended by Antonin Artaud and basic protest against the human condition as outlined in Camus' *The Rebel*.

With *El guerrero ciego* and *La puerta* Rellán has demonstrated that he is, despite his youth and inexperience, one of the foremost writers in Spain today.

12

EDUARDO QUILES

There is nothing unusual about writers being unable to support themselves exclusively by writing. In the United States writers tend to lead fairly comfortable lives as university professors. In Germany there is a tradition of writers working as publishers' editors and readers. In Spain, however, such comparatively comfortable positions are not open to writers—not, in any event, to writers with independent minds. Such writers have to take whatever work they can get, and thus we have the spectacle of one of Spain's leading dramatists, Antonio Martínez Ballesteros, working in an office, or of Eduardo Quiles, who works as a traveling salesman. There are few kinds of life less conducive to creative writing than that of a traveling salesman, yet Eduardo Quiles has managed to write more than thirty plays while covering his territory—the east coast of Spain from his home town of Valencia to Barcelona—for an American pharmaceutical company. Direct support of artists has never been a noticeable characteristic of commercial concerns (indirect support in order to obtain exemption from taxation has, of course, long been a popular public relations device of big business). Consequently Quiles has deemed it advisable to write his plays under the pseudonym of Zacarías Virosque lest his business superiors feel that his sales of pills and capsules are suffering as a result of his creative work. Matters came to a head when Quiles, writing under his own name, won a prize for a television script and had to send his brother to accept the award on the stage of the Teatro Principal

120

of Valencia. Since then he has decided to write openly under his own name, come what may. The decision is a wise one, for his plays will certainly outlast the pharmaceutical company he works for.

Quiles is essentially a metaphysical playwright who portrays man within his social milieu as a means of showing him in his eternal setting. The familiar aspects of Quiles' plots are always gradually revealed as avatars of reality. Quiles' dramatic theory, in other words, is based on Plato's concept of an eternal reality behind the shadow of this life, and it is that *real* or *essential* reality that Quiles portrays through the appearances that, at first glance, we associate with everyday life. At the same time, Quiles has the rare quality of the true dramatist of being able to make these shadows come alive on the stage and hold our interest on their own level. This is not so much a matter of plotting—there is, actually, very little plot and dramatic conflict in Quiles' plays—as of creating characters that are recognizable to the audience and with which it can identify, a much more difficult matter. In identifying with Quiles' shadow characters the audience, of course, is made to realize its own tenuousness.

The tenuousness of human character is dealt with directly in *El hombre y la máscara* ("Man and Mask," 1967), which is basically an exercise in Pirandellian technique. The Author comes on and calls up his characters, and, as in *Six Characters In Search of An Author*, these get away from him and assume a life of their own, arguing with him about the plot and developing personality traits that he never intended them to have. Quiles is not, however, making a comment on the power of artistic inspiration and the subjugation of the creator's will to the products of his imagination, as Pirandello is. As the title of his play suggests, Quiles is concerned with the mutual obscurity of human characters. No one knows the man, only the ever-changing—and capriciously changing—mask. Quiles' point in the play is perhaps best summed up in this quotation from Alexander Lernet-Holenia's *Baron Bagge*: ". . . everyone has only himself to deal with; no one can help another person, and every individual . . . is alone, utterly alone. . . . there are no real relationships between human beings . . . We are always only pretexts for one another, nothing more. Pretexts for hatred or for love. But love and hatred arise within us; they operate in us and pass away again solely within ourselves. No real ties link people together. All that we can ever be to one another is a finer or viler pretext for our own emotions." Lawrence Durrell put it even more starkly in *Justine*: "I realize that each person can only claim one aspect of our character as part of his knowledge. To everyone we turn a different face of the prism." These are truths that we have come to recognize in this century with the destruction of the elaborate comedy played out in the age of Romanticism when sincerity was equated with intensity. Quiles, like the Absurdists, realizes that the human being is a succession of masks, and that the ideal reality behind the shadow is often unknown even to himself.

El hombre y la máscara, because of the excessive reliance on Pirandellian technique, is Quiles' weakest play in the dramatic, though not in the philosophical sense.

El asalariado ("The Employee," 1969) is a far more mature play dramatically. Using the theme of the exploitation of the human being in the business world that Ballesteros uses so effectively in plays like *El pensamiento circular* and *Los mendigos*, Quiles has written a trenchant satire on dehumanization in a computerized society. The scene is an office presided over by the director of the company. His secretary, who doubles as the heroine of his sexual fantasies, helps him in the practical aspects of running the company while the theoretical ones are taken care of by a robot. As the play opens, they are in the process of hiring the employee, who is abjectly ready to debase himself in order to get the job of tending the robot. The action rapidly assumes surrealistic overtones within the basically naturalistic framework of the play. The director has sadomasochistic tendencies and power fantasies, and the employee has "impotent reactions" to everything that goes on around him. Quiles skilfully develops the relationships between the characters until we realize that the employee and the director are the shadow representations of the eternal human dichotomy between the domineering and the domineered—the Idea of Master and the Idea of Slave. The relationship is reminiscent of that between Nebuchadnezzar and his "footstool" in Dürrenmatt's *An Angel Comes to Babylon*. Every millenium or so there is a reversal of the roles as revolutions occur, but the relationship continues. Power corrupts whoever seizes it. The secretary is the necessary sycophantic attribute that all representatives of Power require. But the real source of power is now the Robot-Computer, to which all actual functions are delegated while the ostensible representative of Power preens and playacts. At the end of the play the real source of Power in the modern world is revealed as three faceless, anonymous men, dressed like American gangsters of the 1920's, the representatives of a bigger industrial syndicate that is absorbing the director's company, come in and worship the robot after taking over the business. With the deification of the robot brutal humanity is replaced by inhumanity.

In *El hombre-bebé* ("The Man-Baby," 1969), perhaps his best play, Quiles writes of the way in which people are formed from earliest childhood into the mold that they will occupy the rest of their lives. Free will is an illusion, for as soon as he is born Man's nature and actions are determined. The play opens with Man in his cradle surrounded by the influences that will shape him. There are two angels, good and bad, to indoctrinate guilt feelings in him by rote, and a chorus of relatives to instill social quiescence by setting him acceptable expectations to fulfill. No reasons are given—that would be fatal. Everything is done by rote and by hypnotic suggestion. Man grows up within a social context into which he is expected to fit and which has itself grown by accretion until it constitutes a set of values founded on tradition rather than reason. Man is never permitted to grow up at all, in fact. As the title indicates, he remains a baby, that is, a sentient being reacting to stimuli. From the beginning his path is mapped out for him by people who had their paths mapped out for them. In his turn each Man-Baby is absorbed into the system and becomes a representative of it. As he grows, he is subjected to constant observation in order to keep him devoid of initiative. Once he is grown, he has, in effect, become the sum of the stimuli to which he was subjected, and he continues the process with the next generation. Quiles' play consists of a series of vignettes in which we see this process taking place and climaxing in the graduation speech—a garble of tag-ends of philosophy, none of them logically connected, all of them learned by rote, the whole greeted with fatuous complacency by the listening chorus of relatives who are welcoming the fusion of another limb on to the body social and politic.

With this superbly written panoramic play Quiles has dramatized one of the most significant theories of contemporary sociology. He achieves this through his metaphoric equation of the structure of society with the structure of the body, for just as the form of the grown man's body is predestined from birth and just as he will in turn pass the characteristics of that body on, so the form of his mind is equally predestined and will be passed on to fit the mold in which he was raised and into which he was fused. To be poured into a mold and then cast out is, possibly, to be liberated; but to become the mold itself is to be brainwashed and lost forever. Such is the bleak view of man's destiny that Quiles gives us.

In his two connected short plays *El balón* ("The Ball," 1971) and *El regreso de Dimitri Goss* ("The Return of Dimitri Goss," 1971) Quiles writes the modern version of the Roman "bread and circuses" formula. The modern "circus" to keep the populace quiescent is sports, an anodyne as widely taken in the United States and elsewhere as in Spain. Spain, of course, is unique among the world's countries in having preserved (and passed on to some of its former colonies) a form of gladiatorial contest in the bullfight, but Quiles' target in these plays is football, a much more popular pastime. Bellido used the game as an image of war in his *Football*; Quiles uses it as an image of brainwashing in these two plays.

A visitor from an unspecified foreign country, Dimitri Goss, interested in getting to know the people of the countries he visits on a person-to-person basis, drops into a private club in the (unspecified) country he is visiting. The reading room of the club is dominated by a pedestal with a gigantic football on it before which everyone makes a slight reverence as he enters. Trophies and pictures of athletes line the walls, and all the members are absorbed in reading sporting magazines when they are not in the other room watching movies of football games. Every so often a voice over a loudspeaker tells them of current attractions in the movie room. The club as a whole is a picture of the deviation of interests to trivialities that is so useful to governments intent on remaining in power. Television performs the same function, of course, as it mesmerizes its audience into sitting in slack-jawed hebetude before the functional icon. At the end of *El balón* there is a black-out, and when the lights come up again the gigantic football has been replaced by a book. The voice screams in panic, ordering the members not to bow down before it, but they do so, automatically, without noticing the difference.

In the sequel the troublesome tourist is back again to find the club membership sadly depleted, the book having apparently finally had some effect. The members are leafing through the journals apathetically, and the voice over the loudspeaker pleads with Goss to mind his own business and concentrate on the country's historical monuments and sunny beaches instead of interfering in its internal life. Goss succeeds in enticing two more members away, and the play ends with the voice exhorting the remaining members to stand firm and uphold the traditions, i.e., to remain drugged with their opiate and refrain from doing anything that might affect the life of the nation. Quiles' two plays are a comment on the type of mentality that turns to the sports pages of the newspaper first and usually stops at them, discussing the inanities reported there with the assiduity and seriousness they should be devoting to the news pages.

In *¿Quién es Romo?* ("Who is Romo?" 1971), which, excepting *El hombre-bebé*, is his best play, Quiles has written a cleverly disguised modern morality play in which Natural Man tries to save Riches from perdition and, of course, fails. A prim, prissy man, Pliston, finds Romo, a tramp, sleeping on a park bench one fine morning. Romo seems to be interested in nothing but the songs of the birds and the feeling of things growing around him, thus instantly arousing the reforming instinct in Pliston. Pliston is, according to his own description, a specialist in human problems, a reformer of character, and he cannot abide any sloppiness in the world around him. Romo's way of living outrages him since Romo is an excrescence that does not fit into the neat scheme of society that Pliston worships. His cogitations are interrupted by an agitated friend of his, Classo, a man married to an enormously rich wife who is now threatening to divorce him if he does not bring back the household's butler, who has disappeared. As a specialist in the solution of human problems Pliston is put on his mettle by this situation and he solves it brilliantly by transforming Romo into a butler. In the next scene Romo enchants the spoiled and self-indulgent wife with outrageous flattery and persuades her to get out of her mephitic bedroom and embark on a course of cultural study. Fascinated by the novelty of this approach, the wife is soon completely under Romo's thumb and begins distributing her colossal wealth to various worthy causes in accordance with his instructions. Classo, who began by hugging himself with glee at his wife's pleasure in the new butler, is now panic-stricken at seeing his wife's money frittered away this way, and he calls in Pliston to set the matter right again. Pliston hauls up the standard arsenal of arguments about the disruption of society, the ludicrousness of one person attempting to remedy all the evils of the world, the necessity of doing everything in a well-ordered manner through proper channels, and the inevitability of class distinctions. Romo gives up to return to the natural life, the wife slips easily back into the irresponsible lassitude from which she was momentarily drawn by the attraction of novelty, Classo is once more in full possession of the unearned money that enables him to indulge in his stock market games and luxuries, and Pliston preens himself on the success of "reason," which he fancies that he represents.

In *¿Quién es Romo?* Quiles has produced a brilliant morality play on the basic hypocrisies of modern society. Romo is the natural man close to his chthonic roots, full of selfless instincts but without the deviousness that would enable him to have an effect in the modern world. His naïveté is at once his distinction and his ruin. Pliston is the man of society *par excellence*. He is the voice of reason in the service of convention, mouthing platitudes to order, fatuously self-satisfied and fully convinced of the high-mindedness of the principles he espouses so facilely. He is the organization man who has superseded the natural man in a controlled society which he unconsciously supports as a time-serving lackey. Classo represents the rapacity and brutishness of the businessman who believes that all is his by right although he has earned nothing by honest work, and he is ready for any self-abasement necessary to keep his wealth. His wife represents the very rich of this world who, as Hemingway, echoing Fitzgerald, pointed out, are "different"—the difference lying in their dehumanization and total irretrievability.

Los faranduleros ("The Strolling Players," 1971) combines the themes of *El hombre y la máscara* and *¿Quién es Romo?* in that it is about both the failure of the "natural" man in the modern world and the tragic necessity of wearing masks in order to survive in it. The story concerns a two-man troupe of strolling players whose leader, Braulio, is content to live from hand to mouth as his forefathers did before him, providing entertainment in small towns and villages. His companion, Hermógenes, longs for money and comfortable life and realizes that the day of the strolling player is past. He persuades Braulio to adopt various masks in an attempt to cash in on his good looks, but each scheme fails because of Braulio's idealism and sincerity. At the end Braulio returns to his hopeless and quixotic task of maintaining and following his ideals of freedom and naturalness, while Hermógenes has to content himself with being a commercial huckster.

With the abandonment of his former pseudonym of Zacarías

Virosque and his emergence under his real name, Eduardo Quiles stands revealed as one of the outstanding and most mature dramatists of the new wave of Spanish theater despite the obstacles that he has had to overcome as a result of living and working in Valencia, far from the center of Spain's theatrical life. In all of his plays there is the mark of the true dramatist—the ability to create living characters— and in *¿Quién es Romo?* and *El hombre-bebé* he has written two of the most trenchant social satires of the modern Spanish drama.

13

THE EXILES: ELIZONDO AND GUEVARA

The Spanish underground drama exists outside Spain as well as in it. Like all countries that undergo a political upheaval resulting in the disappearance of democracy and the institution of censorship, Spain suffered a virtually complete loss of its artists and intellectuals. The vast majority of the Spanish artistic and intellectual community either went into exile or remained silent for years. Indeed, it would not be unfair to say that the pre-Civil War writers were cut off by the upheaval. A few, prominent among whom were Rafael Alberti, Alejandro Casona, and Max Aub, continued their careers in exile, but by and large the new generation that was marked by the appearance of Antonio Buero-Vallejo around 1950 started from scratch after a hiatus of several years in Spanish literary production. The isolation of Spain during those years and the rigid censorship to which it was subjected—far more rigid than now—effectively cut off the new writers from the influence of the older generation in exile. One of the reasons for this—aside from the obvious one of the censorship, of course—was the fact that the exiled authors were scattered far and wide, many of them in the Americas. They consequently lost touch with what was going on in Spain. Though much of their work inevitably continued to be preoccupied with what had happened in Spain, it soon became apparent that they were living in the past and writing about their relationship to a set of conditions that no longer existed. Their exile, in other words, denied them the intimate relationship with their setting that is necessary to the creation of art. Part of this was due to the estrangement and part to their natural inability to accept the *fait accompli* of the new order and to recognize the necessity of working from within the new set of conditions. This, of course, is not to deny that the artists in exile continued to do good work, but to doubt whether this work could have any influential significance for the rising generation.

There exists, however, a younger generation of exiled writers as well. These are writers who fled Spain with their parents at the end of the Civil War, either as children or as very young men, and who, having been brought up in France, have lived in close proximity to events in Spain ever since. The best known writer of this group is Fernando Arrabal, but his affinities are much more with French literature than with his native Spanish.

The exiled author most closely bound up with the Spanish under-ground movement is Martín Elizondo. Elizondo, who is now in his late forties, escaped over the Pyrenees at the end of the Civil War and has lived ever since in France, where he now teaches Spanish at the University of Toulouse. Southern France, especially Toulouse and Bordeaux, has become the principal center of Spanish culture in exile as a result of the large number of refugees who settled there after they had fled over the Pyrenees. Because of their proximity, they have been able to keep in close touch with social developments in their homeland so that the Spanish culture of the area may truly be said to be an adjunct of the culture of Spain rather than a culture-in-exile with its characteristics affected by the culture of the adopted country. Martín Elizondo is one of the principal writers of this adjunct Spanish culture.[1] He is the founder and director of "Los amigos del teatro español," a group devoted to the production of Spanish plays for the exiled population of the area. Most of his own plays have been performed by this group.

Elizondo has written plays both in Spanish and in French, but in whatever language he writes, his plays are invariably concerned with the effect of tyranny on the human being. His most important plays are *Otra vez el mal toro* (1967),[2] *La garra y la dura escuela de los Perejones* ("The Claw and the Painful Lesson of the Perejones," 1966), *De verdugo a verdugo* ("From Executioner to Executioner," 1964), *Pour la Grèce* ("For Greece, 1969), and *La Faim* ("Hunger," 1968).

Pour la Grèce, which was first produced in Toulouse in March, 1970 at the Théâtre Daniel Sorano under the direction of Christian Marc, uses the subjugation of Greece in 1967 by a group of army officers, with viewpoints very similar to those of the army officers who took over Spain in 1939, as the starting point of a play about political tyranny in general. One advantage that the Spanish author in exile enjoys is the ability, which most of us so blandly take for granted, to see events in perspective. The restrictiveness of the Spanish author's view is, to be sure, rapidly relaxing, thanks to the influx of tourists and the consequent uncontrollable dissemination of viewpoints from abroad, but it is nevertheless inevitably second-hand and haphazard. The exile has access to a comparatively free press and is able therefore to observe the frighteningly exact parallels between the situation in his homeland and in countries like Greece and Brazil, that have recently fallen under the heavy and brutalizing hand of a totalitarian military dictatorship with all its tiresomely repeated restrictions on personal freedom and with the channeling of all economic resources into the pockets of the few at the apex of the pyramid. Greece thus has become an image of Spain and of all countries where the desires of the few are placed above the necessities of the many. There is an additional reason for the choice of Greece as the tragic image of freedom immolated on the altar of power: the association that it has with the tradition of freedom and the consequent tragic irony of its present condition. The principal problem that Elizondo felt he faced in writing this play was that of compressing a situation, at once so tremendous, so emotionally charged, and yet so obvious, into the compass of the dramatic form without lapsing into the sedulously didactic or the insultingly hortatory. For the reasonably sophisticated audience nothing is more offensive than to be directly exhorted to a point of view that is already obvious to them—the error of Communist drama—and nothing is more boring than to be lectured at when they already agree. Yet the fact that an educated audience in a democratic country is *a priori* opposed to tyranny cannot be taken as a reason for not writing on that subject. The pressing issues remain, even if we are all more or less in agreement on them. To eliminate them on the ground of obviousness leads directly to the mindless escape drama characteristic of totalitarian countries. The problem then becomes one of how to present the obvious without losing effectiveness, how to move and involve without descending to banalities and gaucherie. Elizondo's solution was an adaptation of the breakdown between audience and performers pioneered by Pirandello in *Each In His Own Way*. Instead of an objective demonstration of conditions in Greece in the form of a straight-line fictitious plot, Elizondo gives us a rehearsal and the discussion of an unspecified play about Greece by a group of actors. The actors, in other words, instead of playing Greek characters in a made-up story illustrating the plight of Greece, are playing actors who are rehearsing a play about Greece. What the audience then sees is a discussion of the conditions of tyranny as they affect a group of people—the actors—just like themselves. The theory is that this will enable them to empathize more strongly with the people who really are suffering under these conditions. It will show, as the director, Christian Marc, put it, that the actors themselves—in their real persons—are as disturbed by the conditions under discussion as the audience (presumably) is and that they are asking themselves the same questions about the nature and structure of society.

A consideration of the success of a play like *Pour la Grèce* as a work of art and of its effectiveness as persuasion forces the critic to enquire into the fundamental principles underlying the nature of the theater. The attempt to break down the barrier between performers and audience is made in the interest of sincerity; and while this sounds praiseworthy enough, it violates the one basic tenet of the theater as an art, which is, precisely, insincerity. It stands in defiance of the most profoundly perceptive observation on the nature of the theatrical experience ever made—Samuel Taylor Coleridge's dictum about the audience's automatic suspension of disbelief. The audience does not need to be drawn into the action of an objectively demonstrated story. Assuming that the story is a valid and well-told one and that the performance is a competent one, it is automatically involved. The attempt to break down that artificial barrier between audience and performers which is, in fact, the essence of theatre, in the interest of greater sincerity has actually the opposite effect since the audience perceives that it is being tricked. The actors are not, in point of fact, appearing in their own persons and discussing how the conditions in Greece—or whatever the subject of the play may be—are affecting them: they are still acting, and the rehearsal of the play that the audience sees is as carefully artificial as the play itself would be. What is produced, therefore, is an insincerity that has nothing to do with the insincerity that lies at the root of theatrical practice. The performance of a play is certainly a trick, but the performance of a Pirandellian "anti-play" is a trick doubled since it is an attempt to trick the audience into believing that they are not being tricked.

Elizondo uses the same technique again in *La Faim*, a play in which he writes passionately of the pain and injustice caused by the unequal distribution of the world's food supply. In both these plays Elizondo reveals himself as a writer of immense power and compassion, qualities in no way obscured by his use of what I consider to be the wrong technique for the theatrical medium. Indeed, the practical effectiveness of Elizondo's work in *Pour la Grèce* was vindicated in great part during the the original run of the play when a group from a Fascist youth organization disrupted one of the performances by throwing tear gas bombs on to the stage and eggs at the walls of the theater. At the same time it should be noted that most of the audience was not at all disturbed by this eruption under the impression that it was all part of the play and that the childishly enraged Fascists were all members of the cast.

Elizondo treats the problem of hunger and unequal distribution of property in a more objective and traditional manner in *La garra y la dura escuela de los Perejones*. The Perejones are a large family of have-nots who are evicted from the ramshackle hut, where they live on the verge of starvation, by the owner of the land, an obscenely grasping old woman—she is described as a centenarian—who, together with a few other plutocrats, owns and therefore rules the whole country. The centenarian is the "claw" of the title in which the Perejones and all like them are grasped and squeezed dry, denied their dignity as human beings, and deprived of all the elementary necessities of life, to say nothing of the pleasures and luxuries. Elizondo's central image in the play, which he uses with devastating irony, is the "science" of statistics, which tells us that everyone earns so and so much and eats so and so much per day but takes no account of the inequities implicit in its inhuman averages. The Perejones, according to the statisticians, each eat half a chicken and two pounds of onions every day, but Perejón is, of course, naïvely surprised and disappointed every day to find that his family gets nothing of the sort, since most of the chickens and onions, to say nothing of the lobsters and caviar, are on the surfeited tables of the "claws" that monopolize everything in the country as if they were superior beings with prior rights to the riches of the earth. While the feeling that this system must be overthrown is implicit in the tone of the play, Elizondo has by no means written a piece of simplistic revolutionary exhortation. Like all true thinkers, he presents no solutions. His thought is critical, cogent, and shot through with a bitter, disillusioned irony that he manages to keep compatible with an evident feeling of compassion for and empathy with his downtrodden family of "Perejones." Where *Pour la Grèce* and *La Faim* were plays that were definitely marked by the broader overview of world events available to the exiled writer, *La garra y la dura escuela de los Perejones* is a play that is typical of the thought of the Spanish underground drama and might have been written by one of the authors still living inside Spain.

Elizondo's most ambitious play, although it is a play so quintessentially Spanish as hardly to be comprehensible to anyone not thoroughly familiar with the land and its history, is *Otra vez el mal toro*. Elizondo uses the bull as a triple symbol in this satiric gibe at revolution and its practitioners. Its savagery represents bloodthirstiness; its maleness that heedless self-assertiveness for its own sake known as *machismo*; and its animalism stupidity. The evil bull that comes again is another one in that long and tiresome roll call of useless conspiracies that mar the history of Spain. Elizondo, like all the other Spanish underground authors, is no revolutionary. He has seen too much violence ever again to believe that anything will be accomplished by it. Revolutionary action disguises itself with words that make it seem idealistic altruism, but it is still self-interested and futile no matter how fine the words and how uplifting the slogans. None of this is stated clearly in the play itself, which Elizondo has kept deliberately vague. In a conscious attempt to go beyond the fantastic qualities of the Valle-Inclán *esperpento*, Elizondo has given his play the amorphous structure of a dream—a dream that becomes a nightmare. The viewpoint of the dreamer constantly changes as well, so that the basic style of the play might be described as a shifting expressionism. In addition, much of the action is conducted in a conscious parody of melodrama to emphasize the futility and the ridiculousness of the revolutionary activities. Elizondo also tries to point to what he sees as the essentially theatrical quality of Spanish life with this parody of melodrama and with the grandiloquence of the language, for he looks upon this theatricality as one of the major defects in Spanish life. Self-conscious pride and the habit of doing things for the sake of the pose involved—"the desire of always offering the spectacle of our own person"—have been the downfall of all Spanish reform movements in Elizondo's eyes. It is this quality that he analyses masterfully in *Otra vez el mal toro*.

Despite the advantage that a writer like Elizondo theoretically enjoys in living in a country where no restrictions are put on his writing or on his sources of information, he is a typical case of the tragedy of the exiled author who, torn from his native roots and unable to let down new ones in his adopted country, feels his artistic impulses thwarted by the frustrations he feels as a result of living in a personal and cultural limbo.

Another interesting and talented Spanish expatriate in France is José Guevara, who was born in the province of Huelva in 1928. Primarily a painter who draws his subjects from his native land, he has had one-man exhibitions in Italy, France, Australia, Iraq, Lebanon, Panama, Uruguay, Argentina, West Germany, Luxemburg, Spain, and the United States. Like Elizondo, Guevara is bilingual and writes in both Spanish and French. *Después de la escalada* ("After the Escalation," 1964) is a play that would not ordinarily attract attention except from those whose political acumen does not go beyond the emotional and who confine their views on the war in Vietnam to simplistic excoriation of the role of the United States. The play is not particularly well organized, the first half depicting a candidate for Congress in an unspecified part of the country who makes naïve remarks about the dissatisfaction of Black voters, and undertakes to see that the son of some friends of his is kept out of Vietnam if they will vote for him and he is elected. The second part shows the son in Vietnam after all with two North Vietnamese prisoners whom he is trying to treat in accordance with the Geneva Convention but who are subsequently brutally murdered by his sergeant. The whole thing reads uncomfortably like a rabidly anti-American agitprop play. But now a curious thing has happened. The play, which was written in the early sixties, has suddenly become prophetic. After the revelations of My Lai and the Pentagon Papers Guevara is no longer a gullible, simple-minded victim of the French left-wing press. The structure and style of the play are not improved, of course, but its content has become truth. What seemed mawkish and sophomoric when it was thought to be fiction has become fact. A whole new concept in dramatic criticism is implied by this. Is the play good if it is well-written? Is it good if it speaks the truth? Can such truths as the ones this play deals with be dramatized in any fashion other than the blunt, propagandistic style in which it is written? If it were written more obliquely, more "artistically," would the truth not be emasculated? Can a play be judged favorably if it is well written but does not speak the truth? The answers to these questions, it seems to me, are central to a valid theory of dramatic criticism, and no drama critic has yet been able to answer them adequately. A play like *Después de la escalada* remains a horrifying documentary, a sort of dramatized newsreel. But if it is not art, is art necessarily irrelevant?

Guevara has also written a play in French, *Les Téléphones* ("The Telephones," 1966), which belongs to the absurdist school. It belongs, specifically, to a subdivision of absurdism in which the image of man's existence is death, personified by an executioner. The use of the executioner figure gives a vision of life sustained at the arbitrary will of greater powers, whose purposes not even the executioner is aware of. This executioner, or sometimes jailer, image has, for obvious reasons, been particularly attractive to the Spanish underground authors, having been used by Elizondo, Sastre, Pedrolo, and López Mozo. The inscrutable higher forces that command the executioners—and their fates as well—are given both cosmic and political attributes, thus killing two birds with one stone. In *Les Téléphones*, for example, Guevara writes of a man condemned to death for exercising his freedom of speech. He is brought into a council room full of telephones to await the outcome of his appeal. Trussed in a sack which will contain his bisected body, he listens as his life is played away impersonally through the telephones. Similarly, in *De verdugo a verdugo* Elizondo writes of an executioner and a condemned man who are digging the latter's grave under the control of impersonal voices coming from a loudspeaker. At the end it is the young condemned man who executes the old executioner and assumes his office.

The blank pessimism of these last two plays sums up the attitude of Guevara and Elizondo, writers in exile, deracinated from the sources of their inspiration and embittered by their cultural isolation.

NOTES

1. The other prominent Spanish dramatist in this area is Manuel Martínez Azaña, a descendant of the Spanish Republican Premier, who teaches at the University of Bordeaux. His plays were unfortunately not available for this study.

2. This play has been translated as "The Evil Bull Rides Again" by Mary Ann Perez. It has not yet been published.

14

CATALAN DRAMA

Unlike the speakers of Spanish in the Western Hemisphere, the Iberian Spaniards are in the habit, somewhat curious to foreign ears, of referring to their native tongue as Castillian rather than as Spanish. The point is well taken and prudent, being a tacit—and tactful—recognition of the fact that Spanish is only one of the indigenous languages of Spain. In the northwest Galician is still very much a live idiom; in the north Basque is spoken as freely as the official language; and in the east Catalan is the vernacular, as it has been for more than eight centuries. Each of these languages has its own literature and each has survived attempts to suppress it. The situation is considerably improved now, but for a period these languages could not be taught in the schools or printed in books. Few projects are more futile than linguistic suppression, and the attempt was foredoomed to failure. Catalan, like Basque and Galician, is now once more flourishing openly, and its literature is undergoing a full scale revival.

Catalan has always had a literary production quite out of proportion to the extent of its linguistic distribution. Spoken by about six million people, largely in the area around Barcelona, along the east coast of Spain, and in the Balearic Islands, Catalan has a literature that is unexpectedly copious, going back at least to the second half of the 11th century.[1] The isolated, hermetic quality that can be observed at various periods in Castillian life and literature has never appeared in Catalan. Catalan society and literature have always been far more cosmopolitan than their Castillian counterparts. For Catalonia there have been no Pyrenees. Stretched out along the open east coast of Spain and reaching out into the Mediterranean to the Balearics and as far east as Sardinia (where a dialect of Catalan is still spoken by the descendants of Catalan settlers in the town of Alghero), Catalonia has always been receptive to outside influences. Linguistically, indeed, its ties are closer to Provençal than to Castillian, and culturally too there is as strong a connection to France as to Spain.

As a fringe language of the Iberian peninsula Catalan, like Galician and Basque, has always been in an embattled position, accentuated by the periodic misguided attempts of the central government to suppress it or to tolerate it at the most as a peasants' vernacular. These attempts were doubly misguided. They were misguided because they were foredoomed to failure since a language can no more be suppressed than a book can; and because, predictably, they had the opposite ultimate effect from the intended one. They served only to consolidate the belief of the Catalonians in their separateness and uniqueness, and served to stimulate a political as well as a linguistic nationalism. The centuries-long struggle to survive as a linguistic and cultural enclave within a political entity has bred a characteristic quality of tenacity and independence among Catalonians that is reflected in a deliberate avoidance of Castillian influence in their literature. Because of this reaction Catalan literature has always been more susceptible to the polyglot influences brought to it by the Mediterranean, and even now, when Castillian literature itself has become a thoroughly European literature, Catalan is still more open to outside influence because of its geographical position. Indeed it might well be argued that the opening up of contemporary Castillian literature to European influences has come through Catalonia.

Catalan drama after the Civil War was no more fortunate than Castillian drama. In fact, its eclipse was even more complete since public performances in Catalan were forbidden. Gradually the Catalan characteristics of survival and tenacity asserted themselves, as private performances in Catalan by and for a few people clandestinely gathered together served to carry on the tradition.[2] During the forties, indeed, Catalan culture had to be maintained in a manner analogous to that of the early Christians in the catacombs. The tenacious hold that Catalan has over its native speakers is illustrated by the fact that cultural considerations assumed primacy at this time over class distinctions. The underground efforts to preserve Catalan culture were largely the work of the bourgeoisie. Thus we find ourselves confronted with the paradox of a class that dominated public affairs, conservative and devoted to its own interests though it may have been, becoming engaged in various cultural activities that they did not ordinarily consider very respectable, among them the theater, through fidelity to a language that they were not disposed to renounce.[3]

The most extraordinary writer to emerge in Catalan literature since the Civil War is Manuel de Pedrolo (b. 1918). Were it not for the fact that Pedrolo writes exclusively in Catalan he would be recognized as one of the world's outstanding contemporary writers. Pedrolo has written extensively in the fields of the novel, the short story, and the drama, but, with the exception of three plays, none of his work has yet been translated into English.[4]

Pedrolo's best plays show very clear signs of absurdist influence. They are all concerned with the basic incomprehensibility of man's relationship to the world around him and his inability to adjust to the conditions of his existence. In form and viewpoint they remind one very strongly of Beckett's *Waiting for Godot* and *Endgame*, and Beckett is undoubtedly the strongest single literary and philosophical influence on Pedrolo. It would be a mistake, however, to classify Pedrolo simply as an imitator of Beckett. Too often, for one thing, authors tend to be dismissed as lacking originality and importance if they can be demonstrated to be imitators of other authors. The line between imitation and influence is, however, a very fine one—in most cases, so fine as to be indistinguishable. In any case, the distinction is purely academic since to be a *successful* imitator of Beckett is to be oneself something very close to a great dramatist. Manuel de Pedrolo is, however, his own man: the "imitation" of Beckett goes no further than a coincidence of vision.

Pedrolo's vision is of a world in which men fight desperately, stubbornly, instinctively to push back the knowledge of the indefinable menace that they feel surrounding them. His favorite image is that of an enclosed space, usually a room. This room is the world to its inhabitants, who feel trapped in it and hate it, but usually have an even greater fear of what is outside. His plays are metaphysical dramas that show humanity stripped down to its essentials. The action of Pedrolo's plays never consists of what we might call social

movement, that is, the recognizable everyday actions of human beings. In many plays, of course, these "social" actions are merely
the outward indication of an inner essence that they represent or
symbolize. In Pedrolo's plays we see the skeletal inner essence:
reality seen bare, without the "clothing" of social movement, unob-
scured by the web of conventional gesture that covers reality and
ameliorates our apprehension of it in everyday life and in ordinary
drama. Pedrolo's plays are set neither in specified time nor place
but in an extraterrestrial ultimate reality where the Platonic essences
of being exist. His plays show us the reality for which the reality we
know is the name. Samuel Beckett is the only other playwright to
have accomplished this transposition effectively. There are, however, certain other obvious analogies that are worth pointing out.
José Monleón has pointed out that Pedrolo's predilection for the
image of the room derives ultimately, as does Pinter's, from Sartre's
No Exit.[5] This is undoubtedly true, but it should be noted that both
Sartre and Pinter use the room or enclosed space image quite dif-
ferently from Pedrolo. In Sartre's play the action, although taking
place in a putative Hell, is completely bound to everyday reality.
No Exit is a psychological drama saying that Hell is within ourselves
and in our relations to other people, those relations consisting of
the outward and superficial manifestations of our inner impulses.
Both Pedrolo and Beckett would have shown the inner emptiness
and stasis which the actions of the characters are an attempt to
disguise. Sartre, in other words, shows us that in order to cover up
the hell of the knowledge of our essential nullity we create a web of
conflicting actions and character traits that constitute a new hell of
misunderstandings, hatreds, and self-loathing. Pinter, on the other
hand, uses the room image as a haven from the world. Pinter's
characters gather in rooms that are womb-like structures where
they cower in embryonic regression, jealously guarding themselves
against invasion from the darkness outside. When they are torn
loose from their cocoons and forced out of their warm, well-lighted
caverns it is at once a birth and a death. In Pedrolo's plays the rooms
are either all that there is—they seem to be floating in a vacuum—or
they are as cold and forbidding as the outside. Like Beckett, Pedrolo
is uncompromising. He holds out no comforting hand.

Cruma (1957) is a play that shows the quintessence of life,
existence pared down to its most skeletal. The scene is a bare room
with blank, white walls. The man who lives there, the "Resident,"

has only a chair and an ashtray. He is visited, as every day, by a friend, the "Visitor." Every day these two do something different to distract themselves and keep out the memory of the past, the threat of the present, and the dread of the future. This time when the Visitor enters he finds the Resident measuring the walls. This is the "game for today"—the thing that they must do to keep out thought. This obsession of theirs is rather reminiscent of the "old jokes" and the attempted hanging in *Endgame* and *Waiting for Godot*, just as the Visitor's warning that the appearance of the ashtray (it was not there the day before) presages an inundation of inanimate objects and thus a violation of the skeletal purity in which they live and which they try to preserve with the jealous and self-absorbed care of men tiptoeing on eggshells recalls Ionesco's *The New Tenant*. The game the two men play turns out to be a flop, for they find that the numbers have disappeared from their tape measures, which are now completely blank. They cannot measure the room anymore, i.e., they cannot make any sense of their world. The world did, perhaps, make sense once when it was simpler and the products of technology and thought had not yet encroached on human life so completely. "Cruma" is the name of an Etruscan unit of measurement, which, like everything else Etruscan, is lost to us. The world the Etruscans knew could, perhaps, have been measured or understood by them, but the world as it is cannot be measured or understood by us. Another aspect of the play is the Resident's inability to relate to other people. His world is enclosed by the walls of his room. He is, as it were, a monad floating through existence unaware of the other particles he meets. People pass through his room to an inner room, where, he tells his friend, all are dead, but he cannot distinguish these people and insists they are "nobody." When the Visitor goes to the bathroom a completely different man, the "Stranger," comes out, but nothing will convince the Resident that this is another person. If he did admit the difference he would have to relate to another person, and that would mean breaking his carefully constructed cocoon and letting chaos in. Pedrolo's depiction of the Resident's life and character shows us his vision of what each person's life really is at the core: a struggle to maintain the pitifully minimal amount of personal autonomy he has by living in as self-centred a way as possible.

In *Sóc el defecte* ("I Am the Defect," 1959) Pedrolo shows us Man outside the Room. The world outside the cocoon is depicted in its essential form as a maze of staircases, and as one sees it one feels a certain retrospective sympathy with the Resident for guarding his fortress so jealously. If the alternative to the stark, bare room is this labyrinth, then perhaps the Resident was right in hugging to himself his feeling of inviolability and the precarious balance within his interior world that it gave him.

The active principle in *Sóc el defecte* is represented by Ar and Ber, who constantly go up and down the steps trying to make sense out of their activities by minutely examining the meanings of the words "climb" and "descend." Since the meaning of the words is relative to their position on the steps at any particular moment, they never do find any meaning. Similarly, Cir, who sits at the bottom of one of the staircases with a pile of books around him, never finds any meaning through his espousal of the mental principle in life either. He soaks up knowledge—the pages of the books he reads become blank because everything on them is transferred to his mind—but he finds out no more than Ar and Ber do with their eternal trudging up and down the stairs. Two girls, Dor and Fur, come in and want to play ball with the men. They realize that only play makes any sense in life because the meaning of life is relative to us and we are in flux:

AR: Do you mean that we can't find it?
DOR: I don't know. It won't do you any good to find it . . . or to believe that you've found it.
AR: Why?
DOR: Because everything is provisional.
FUR: And subjective.
DOR: Afterwards you'll die.
FUR: And the others will have to start all over again.
AR: But I . . .
DOR: You can only search for yourself—and you're nothing. You're nobody.
AR: But if I find . . .
DOR: The discovery ends with you . . . if that's what it is. Because you can never be sure.
FUR: There's no point of reference. Just you, and you're changing, modifying, growing old. The point of reference is moving.
DOR: You'll just be fooling yourself.
FUR: Because you're a self-deluding animal subject to egoistic

satisfactions and self-interested illusions, imprisoned between two white milestones enclosing a transient world.

DOR: Don't you see that it's impossible to build upon shifting sand?

The men realize the emptiness of life and try to find consolation: "We're alive . . . and we have to wait till we die." The similarity of viewpoint between this play and *Waiting for Godot* or *Endgame* is immediately apparent, but it should be emphasized that Pedrolo has written no slavish imitation but an original drama on the same subject and with the same *Weltanschauung*.

The characters in *Sóc el defecte* are outside, but they are as firmly imprisoned within the narrow possibilities that their lives offer them as the Resident in *Cruma*. The Resident wants to remain imprisoned, and Ar and Ber come to realize that they cannot escape the maze.

In *Tècnica de cambra* (*The Room*, 1959), however, there is no thought of escape: the room *is* the world, *is* life.[6] The scene is a dormitory room in a hostel. Miscellaneous objects are scattered about. One by one, seven young people—three men and four women —are introduced into the room by an invisible landlady whose voice can be heard fulsomely praising the comforts of the room. The seven people are different types of humanity—domineering, submissive, selfish, and so on. They are not caricatures in any sense, however. As they come in, each carries an empty suitcase, preempts a space in the room and some objects from the shelves, and settles down. But this room is the world, and there are neither enough beds nor enough objects (one of which is a knife) to go round. What Pedrolo shows us here with consummate dramatic skill is a microcosm of life and its conflicts played out in the compass of this ordinary room. At the end the characters are called out of the room by the voice of the landlady, just as they were introduced, one by one. They leave, for they have no choice, some reluctantly, some resignedly, discarding their earthly dross—the tinsel of objects they have acquired by barter or violence—as they go. At the end the room is empty again, but the eternal cycle of life begins again as we hear the voice of the landlady lauding the room to a new tenant. *The Room* is a bold experiment, for the representation of life as a whole in everyday terms runs the danger of becoming trite, but Pedrolo succeeds in making the dramatic image into which he has compressed his view of life a valid and workable one. To the cynical mind life as a brief stay in a seedy hotel room has its attractions.

The room is again a symbol, though not of the world or of life this time, in *Darrera versió, per ara* ("Last Version, Up to Now," 1958).[7] Once again we have the bare white room with no furniture except a sphere painted half black and half white. There are two closed doors and a window looking out on a void. A young man and a young woman, the latter restless and dissatisfied, are waiting or living in this room. They are aimless and bored. "Have you noticed that 'nothing' is the word we use more than any other?" the woman asks. They have rented the room but are dissatisfied with the conditions of the lease, one of which is that they cannot leave the room. Nor do they care for the black and white sphere, which does not belong to them. The faintly sinister landlady (she seems to materialize outside the window) is no help when summoned, although she says it is her function to serve them. They cannot break their lease, she tells them, nor should they want to, since they have "everything" in the room. As for the sphere, although they may look on its presence as an imposition, she has entrusted it to them as a sign of her confidence in them. She cannot make any changes in the terms of the lease because she herself is not free. To their complaints that she constantly spies on them she replies that if they did not have anything to hide they would not mind. After a while they are visited by a neat, well-spoken young man carrying an all-white sphere who urges them to be satisfied with the room and obey the rules, and by a bearded Bohemian who rolls an all-black sphere around and who urges them to take their sphere and clear out. By now it has become clear that Pedrolo is writing a parable of the Fall. The bare white room with the spy hole is the Garden of Eden; the two visitors with their symbolic spheres, angel and devil; and the landlady a Deity in the grip of a determinism inexplicable even to Itself. Adam and Eve decide to take their sphere, with its equal potential for good and evil, and leave. In the next scene they have set up housekeeping in a modest little apartment and are building their own lives, independent of any outside influence, having rejected both angel and devil. The play skirts the borderline of the obvious rather closely but is saved by the conclusion, in which Pedrolo has turned a religious parable into an affirmation of the primacy of humanity. In the end, when the couple rejects both angel and devil, it is as if these had never existed. In the act of rebellion itself, as Camus has shown, the supernatural is negated. Man is the architect of his own fate and has no need of the crutches offered him by a worn out mythology that ceases to exist the moment it is no longer believed in.

The plays discussed so far have been concerned, virtually exclusively, with metaphysical matters. In them Pedrolo has concentrated on expounding his profoundly pessimistic and mordant conception of man and his place in the universe. Both in form and content they remind one of Beckett. In *Homes i No* ("Men and No," 1957), *Situació bis* (*Full Circle*, 1958), and *L'ús de la matèria* ("The Use of Matter," 1963) Pedrolo uses the absurd form for political as well as metaphysical purposes. *Homes i No* uses a cage metaphor rather than the usual room. There are two cages or cells on stage. In each reside a family—husband, wife, and child. They have always lived in these cages, guarded by a man named No who lives in the narrow passage between their cages. They try desperately to get out—through the bars, over them, through the floor, or by overpowering No. Nothing works. At the end the curtains behind the cages are drawn back to reveal more bars guarded by more men. Their jailer, No, is himself imprisoned and so on, presumably ad infinitum. At first glance this would seem to be a supremely pessimistic work from either the philosophical or the political viewpoint; and indeed it would be legitimate to interpret the work in this way, as José Monleón has done.[8] If we assume that behind the previously unsuspected bars revealed at the end there stretches an infinite series of bars, then the play demonstrates a total pessimism. The author himself has suggested, however, that it was not his intention to postulate an infinite series of bars, but to suggest that the series is finite, that the defeat of No and the revelation of the bars behind him is a step forward. The defeat of No in the play is engineered by the two children, using methods that their parents had never thought to use. Through the defeat of No they have been brought together and will presumably produce children who in their turn will break down the next series of bars until human freedom will finally be won.[9]

Full Circle is actually a much more pessimistic play than *Homes i No*. In this play the scene is a prison-like courtyard with individual rooms around it. In the middle of the yard is a large bin. At stated times a bell rings, everyone returns to his room, and two robot-like characters come through the gates, one carrying a stick, the other a sack. The man with the sack, which is full of letters, empties it into the bin. As soon as they depart the inmates burst out of their rooms and grab as many letters as they can. This seems to be at one and the same time the only pleasure and the purpose of their lives. Between mail deliveries they are virtually in a state of suspended animation. One day one of the inmates decides to question the rules and to try and find out why things are the way they are. With great difficulty he persuades his companions to rebel by refusing to read the letters. Finally they find it necessary to kill the messengers, and the rebel leader and one other go out to find out what it is all about. When they come back, however, they have been transformed into new editions of the messengers and vouchsafe no explanations but only reaffirm the previous rules. Life still depends on the bell and the letters, and the messengers from outside must neither be seen nor be spoken to. The taste of rebellion and victory has been too heady for the other inmates, however, and they refuse to obey. The two messengers trick each of their old friends and companions in rebellion into returning to his room for a talk, whereupon they follow and murder them one by one. At the end they are left alone, possessors of the supreme power they came to crave but with no one to exercise it on.

Although the outside power, which is never defined, has certain of the characteristics of God or of an all-controlling cosmic malignity, *Full Circle* is primarily a powerful political parable, in which Pedrolo speaks of the corruptive effect of power and of the faithlessness of political victors to the ideals for which they fought. Political revolutionaries are like Cronus, swallowing their children lest they in turn be deposed. Their rebellion founders on the reef of their own insecurity and insincerity, both malleable raw materials in the process of conversion from pristine idealism to the moral putrefaction that the possession of power brings. As the disappointed rebel leader in Genet's *The Balcony* remarks after it is all over, "No truth was possible."

L'ús de la matèria is basically as serious as Pedrolo's other plays, but it is written in the form of a hilarious farce. The scene is an office where two minor government bureaucrats spend their lives signing papers and quoting the hundreds of regulations by which they live. In its satire of bureaucracy the play is worthy of standing with Vaclav Havel's *The Memorandum*. It is full of inspired pieces of nonsense like the plan of one of the two clerks to have specialists not merely in signing names, but in crossing t's, dotting i's, and writing each letter of the alphabet. In this way everyone will be brought into the bureaucratic machine and no one will any longer have to suffer the horrible fate of being an "outsider." At another point they are ordered to destroy all the papers that clutter their office from floor to ceiling in the interest of efficiency and tidiness—but of course, they must retain a copy and a duplicate of each paper they destroy!

In all of his plays Pedrolo attempts to create an image of the world or of human life in terms of its essentials and to make this image dramatically viable. In the plays discussed here he has been outstandingly successful. Were it not for the obscurity of the language in which he writes he would long ago have been recognized as one of the leading dramatists of the absurdist theatre.[10]

There can be no question of Manuel de Pedrolo's supremacy in the Catalan drama. The only man to come close to him as a writer is Salvador Espriu, and he is primarily a poet. By far the most promising younger Catalan dramatist is Josep Benet i Jornet (b. 1940). Benet's most significant plays are *Cançons perdudes* ("Lost Songs," 1966), *La nau* ("The Ship," 1969), and *Marc i Jofre o els alquimistes de la fortuna* ("Marc and Jofre or The Alchemists of Fortune," 1968).[11]

Xavier Fábregas, the leading scholar and critic of Catalan literature, has pointed out that one of the principal themes of the modern Catalan drama is the problem of Catalan identity.[12] The preservation of the language and the native cultural tradition is seen as the key in the struggle to maintain a sense of belonging to a separate ethnic entity, if not a political one. In *Cançons perdudes* Benet creates a fable of an imaginary country, Drudania, that, like Catalonia, is hemmed in on all sides by a foreign country and by the sea, and that is governed by an emissary of an external power. Benet's purpose in writing this play, which, although well-written, is inevitably of secondary interest to non-Catalonians, was to make a comment on the manner in which Catalan culture is being preserved. As has already been noted, the revival of Catalan culture after the Civil War was largely in the hands of the bourgeoisie. Their motives were, for the most part, based on an unwillingness to see their vernacular language die out and on a dilettantistic appreciation of the indigenous culture. In other words, their primary concern was with their own businesses and with their own lives in a world that basically had nothing to do with Catalan culture. They approached that culture, therefore, in an objective manner, as something quaint and folkloristic but not as something with which they were organically connected and which had roots in their own inner beings. The peasantry and the working class, on the other hand, were too busy with the simple act of survival to care, and the latter, in any case, was being diluted by an enormous influx of immigrant labor, principally from Andalusia. Benet's conclusion in the play is that there is no longer any point in trying to recreate the past, and that the culture must be preserved by developing the country and by creating new art that is at once genuinely representative of current Catalan thought and true to its traditions without being deliberately antiquarian.

Marc i Jofre again takes up the myth of Drudania in order to speak about contemporary political matters. It takes place in some unspecified period of the past, probably the Middle Ages, and is set within a frame story set in the present. The main action of the play, in fact, purports to be the story of a romantic novel that is being read by a character in the frame story. This plot is a typical romantic fairy tale replete with sinister usurper, mysterious paternity, intrigues, chases, and all the rest of the paraphernalia to which Sir Walter Scott's novels have accustomed us.[13] The point of all this is that political conflicts will never be resolved through artists, intellectuals, gentlemen, love, or Machiavellian diplomacy, each of which is represented by a character in the play, but by the instinctive chthonic force of the people as a whole. The solution thus presented is hardly new and hardly workable in its vague idealism. The significant aspect of this extremely well-written and well-constructed play surely lies in the author's assertions as to where the solution does not lie—in his categorical rejection of the traditional sources of political solutions.

Cançons perdudes and *Marc i Jofre* are both set in Drudania, Benet's mythical counterpart of Catalonia, and are concerned primarily with Catalan problems. In Benet's best play to date, *La nau,* the Drudania myth is still used, but the play is far more wide-ranging in its application than the other two. In *La nau* Benet uses the conventions of science-fiction as his framework. The "ship" of the title is an enormous spaceship containing a million people on its way from Earth (Drudania) to colonize the farthest stars. Like Pedrolo in *Darrera versió, per ara*, Benet has constructed a parable based on the Fall of Man. In Pedrolo's play the existential act of breaking the lease on the barren apartment brought freedom and peace—and the equal possibility of good and evil through further existential acts. In Benet's view the Fall has given a group of unscrupulous business entrepreneurs the opportunity to control all men by playing on their belief and on their feelings of guilt and fear. The spaceship *is* the world, and the Fall consisted of its blast-off. The Earth was the Garden of Eden and in seeking to leave it and discover the secret of the universe by trying to reach the stars, where the Spirit resides, men fell from grace—or so they are told by the entrepreneurs to whom they have fallen victim. When the play opens, many centuries have already passed in the spaceship. A funeral service is in progress during which the priest (here called a Technician) reads from the Holy Book, which recounts how men rebelled in building the Ship to reach the stars where the Spirit resides. As a result, the Spirit abandons them. After many years a group of Technicians enters the engine room and kills the Scientists (freethinkers) who began the voyage. They pray to the Spirit, who answers them and says that the Engine Room shall henceforth be the Holy of Holies which only the Technicians may enter; and nobody may touch the levers that control the movement of the Ship except the Head Technician, to whom the Spirit will give His direct instructions. The parable of the expulsion from the Garden of Eden and the rise of religion is clear enough in this science fiction version of Benet's. His purpose is to show how the Technicians have taken over the lives of the million inhabitants of the Ship by playing on their fears and by pretending to be omniscient.

The man with whose funeral the play opens is given out as a suicide but has actually been murdered by the Technicians because he penetrated to the Engine Room. Once an ordinary mortal has penetrated to the Engine Room he must be eliminated lest he tell his fellow men the secret of the Holy of Holies—which is that there is nothing there, of course. The protagonist of the play also penetrates to the Engine Room in the course of investigating his friend's death, and he, too, will presumably be killed. But before this happens he moves the one lever which shows signs of having been used, the others all being rusted into immobility. The lever opens a window in the side of the Ship revealing the infinite spaces of the sky—i.e., revealing the reality that has been kept hidden from the people by the Technicians. Allegorically speaking, the Ship is the world closed off and bounded by the arbitrary rules of religion and government. When Dan opens the window at the end, he opens up the possibilities of the mind of man unfettered by the restrictions of tradition. The window looks out upon the cold, bare spaces where only existential freedom is possible, and where neither religion nor repressive government has any place—where there is no place for the manipulations of the technicians who make the human psyche their field of operations.

With *La nau* Josep Benet has established himself as one of the most promising playwrights in both Spanish and Catalan and has demonstrated his ability to write plays whose meaning reaches far beyond the native culture he treats in *Cançons perdudes* and *Marc i Jofre*.

Although Manuel de Pedrolo is without a doubt the best Catalan writer in the dramatic medium active in our time, and although Josep Benet is the most promising of the numerous young Catalan dramatists who are just now beginning to appear, they are by no means alone. There are several other dramatists of importance or potential importance writing in Catalonia today. Writers like Alexandre Ballester, Joan Soler, Joan Colomines, Feliu Formosa, Jordi Teixidor, Baltasar Porcel, Xavier Romeu, Jaume Melendres, Jordi Dodero, and Jordi Bayona have all written works of interest. Josep María Muñoz Pujol has written a version of the Antigone legend (*Antígona*, 1965) [14] that makes Anouilh's version, which it resembles superficially, seem facile and shallow in comparison. María Aurèlia Capmany, a well-known novelist before she turned to the theater and helped Ricard Salvat found the Adrià Gual School of Dramatic Art in Barcelona, has written an excoriation of the listlessness of the Catalan bourgeoisie in the face of the century's disasters in *Vent de garbí i una mica de por* ("Southwest Wind and A Little Fear," 1965). [15] And, finally, Ricard Salvat himself, the leading spirit of the contemporary Catalan theater and one of the foremost directors in Europe, has adapted texts of Catalonia's greatest living writer, Salvador Espriu, for the stage in *Ronda de Mort a Sinera* ("Dance of Death in Sinera," 1966). [16] All of these works and all of these writers together constitute one of the major dramatic literatures of the world today.

1. Joan Gili, *Introductory Catalan Grammar* (Oxford: Dolphin Book Co., 1952), p. 83.

2. Xavier Fábregas, *Teatre Català d'agitació política* (Barcelona: Edicions 62, 1969), p. 271.

3. *Ibid.*, p. 272.

4. The three plays are *Situació bis*, translated by B. D. Steel as *Full Circle* in *Modern International Drama*, IV, i (1970), *Cruma*, translated by the present writer but as yet unpublished, and *The Room* (cf. note 6, below).

5. Manuel de Pedrolo, *Hombres y No*, translated by José Corredor Matheos (Barcelona: Aymá, 1966), p. 15.

6. Published in *Modern International Drama*, V, ii (1972). Originally published by Editorial Moll in Palma de Mallorca in 1964.

7. Published by Edicions 62 in Barcelona in 1971.

8. *Hombres y No*, p. 23.

9. *Ibid.*, pp. 129–130.

10. There is a brief treatment of Pedrolo's *Cruma* and *Homes i No* in Martin Esslin's *The Theatre of the Absurd*.

11. *Marc i Jofre* was published by Edicions 62 in Barcelona in 1970; *Cançons perdudes* was published in a volume entitled *Fantasia per a un auxiliar administratiu* by Editorial Moll in Palma de Mallorca in 1970.

12. Fábregas, *op. cit.*, pp. 291–292.

13. Benet specifically acknowledged the influence of Scott in a letter to the present writer.

14. Published by Aymá in Barcelona in 1967.

15. Published by Editorial Moll in Palma de Mallorca in 1968.

16. Published by Barrigotic/Grafiques Gravil in Barcelona in 1966.

15

OTHER PLAYWRIGHTS

It would not be unfair to say that the principal theme of this book has been the extraordinary manner in which the best authors of the current Spanish theater have stubbornly continued to write in the face of difficulties that have traditionally discouraged dramatic authors and forced them either to remain silent in their hopelessness or to change their writing to other genres. Not only have these authors obstinately refused to budge from what they conceive to be their métier and their task as artists, they have continued to write plays with an abandon that would make them seem prolific even if they were sure of having everything they wrote produced. It is, however, inevitable under such circumstances that some writers feel restricted and produce less than they otherwise might. This chapter is concerned with a number of such authors—writers who have produced only one or two plays, although the quality and maturity of those plays indicates that they might be capable of more if the conditions under which they wrote were not so limiting. The tragedy inherent in the present theatrical situation in Spain is twofold, consisting as much in the plays that are not being written as a result of the discouragement felt by the authors as in the plays that are being written and then allowed to rot in oblivion.

One of the authors of potential major quality who has been affected by these circumstances is Ramón Gil Novales, born in Huesca in 1926 and now living in Barcelona. His first play was *La hoya* ("The Grave," 1966), which I have not had an opportunity to examine. In 1969 the students of the Adrià Gual School of Dramatic Art in Barcelona produced *Guadaña al resucitado* ("Scythe to the Resurrected"), which had been written in 1966.[1] This play is one of the strongest and most uncompromising statements of social justice in the modern theater. The principal landowner and political boss of a remote village somewhere in Spain is on the point of dying. Virtually all the land in the village and in the surrounding area belongs to him, and by leasing it out to the villagers on the share-cropping principle he has kept them in a state of near slavery. The appearances of self-government are preserved—there is a village council and a mayor, but since they are all dependent on the land-owner for their continued subsistence, he is, in fact, the law in the whole area. Such conditions still exist in Spain, particularly in Andalusia, where the system of *latifundia*—enormous landholdings embracing several villages—is still maintained. Nor is the system peculiar to Spain. The kind of barely concealed slavery that Gil Novales depicts in this play can still be found all over the world, although it is not always based on land. When the landowner dies, he leaves the peasants a document willing them the land. The peasants, free at last, divide up the land among themselves and proceed to show themselves perfectly capable of living as free men and governing themselves. The landowner's will turns out to be his last trick on the men off whom he has lived and whom he has always despised. His son shows up with a document of later date leaving everything to him, so that the peasants, after their brief taste of freedom and property, are back where they started. The brief taste was a heady one as well, however, for the next scene involves the arrival of an investigative judge come to look into the mysterious disappearance of the landowner's son. Gil Novales displays a fine sense of the dramatic here by going directly from the peasants' disillusion and despair at the appearance of their new slavedriver to the investigation of his disappearance instead of showing us the act of revenge itself. The villagers put an absolutely solid front up to the judge and immovably deny everything, slyly mocking him on his inability to discover anything. The end result is that the judge has to go without having accomplished anything, leaving the peasants in possession of their land, and the man who tried to take it away from them without having done a stroke of work for it, in possession of his unknown grave. Students of the Spanish drama in its previous Golden Age will have no difficulty is assigning Gil Novales' inspiration to Lope de Vega's *Fuenteovejuna*, of course. Essentially what Gil Novales has done in *Guadaña al resucitado* is to adapt Lope's play to modern times. In doing so he has lost none of the power of the original, having, in fact, created an entirely new play on the theme of the old.

Since writing *Guadaña al resucitado* Gil Novales has turned to the novel in discouragement at the theatrical situation in Spain, a course which, if he persists in it, will result in the loss of a potentially major dramatic talent.

The experience of Carlos Pérez Dann (b. 1936) has been similar to that of Gil Novales. Like him, Pérez Dann has apparently ceased to write for the stage after showing a great deal of promise. His two most impressive plays to date are *Mi guerra* ("My War," 1966) and *El insaciable Peter Cash o los cuernos de la abundancia* ("The Insatiable Peter Cash or The Horns of Plenty," 1970).[2]

Mi guerra is an anti-war satire that is to some degree reminiscent of the style of Martínez Ballesteros in *The Best Of All Possible Worlds* and *The Straw Men*. Unlike most American anti-war playwrights, Pérez Dann imbues his work with black humor rather than with strident indignation, and his play achieves a correspondingly more powerful effect. *Mi guerra* is written in the style of a grotesque clown show about an imaginary war in which the President of one of the countries involved has to satisfy his mania for "honor" and "glory" by giving medals to the office cleaners since his army is not producing any heroes. The paucity of *bona fide* heroes is the result of the fact that the opposing armies are currently at a stalemate. Fighting has gradually been tapering off as more and more people on each side have been drafted. At first each side very sensibly drafted only people of the lowest intelligence and fighting was hot and heavy, but as the armies ran out of morons, the middle-class was drafted, and finally the intellectuals. At the present time the front lines are occupied exclusively by scholarly types who are far too busy rationalizing cowardice and debating the philosophical aspects of war to do any fighting. Pérez Dann shows this in a scene in which four soldiers crawl into an empty house in the middle of the battlefield and are unable to decide which side they are on. Since they all claim to be fighting for justice and liberty, they decide that they are all on the same side. The war comes to a standstill because even the officers on both sides say they are fighting for liberty and justice. This happens after a little coaxing from the common soldiers, since, being career men rather than draftees, they are not so sure what they are supposed to be fighting for. Appalled at this turn of events, the presidents of the two countries call a summit meeting to find out what is wrong. They hire the world's two greatest politicians to solve the problem. One of them suggests peace as a means of stimulating war since wars only start in peacetime. The rest of their suggestions and arguments are all on this level of intelligence, and the play consequently climaxes in a chaos of puerilities as the two politicians vainly try to find reasons for the soldiers to fight each other. *Mi guerra* tends to fade out toward the end in repetitiveness as Pérez Dann keeps thinking up ways to make his basic point, which is that each side in a war is deluded into fighting by having slightly different versions of the same slogans drummed into it. The play has all the material for an excellent one-act drama such as Ballesteros' *The Straw Men*, which it resembles thematically. This tendency to overwrite is very common among the new Spanish playwrights and, since the basic situations of the plays are frequently of outstanding dramatic quality, must be ascribed once again to the lack of opportunities for production.

The same criticism may be made of Pérez Dann's *El insaciable Peter Cash*, in which he attempts nothing less than a symbolic history of economics. The extraordinary thing about the play is that he almost carries it off. Again one of the defects of the play is overwriting, but what is basically wrong with it is Pérez Dann's mixture of symbolism with realism. Peter Cash, who, of course, symbolizes money, is depicted in so realistically human a manner that the reader (like most new Spanish plays, this one has not yet had any spectators) all too often forgets that he is merely a symbol. It is essential for a proper understanding of the author's point that the reactions of the other characters to Peter Cash are clearly the reactions of human beings to money. At the same time it must be admitted that Pérez Dann's inspiration of making Peter Cash a Don Juan type who is absolutely irresistible to women is a brilliant one— the best possible if money is to be shown as a personified symbol. The play takes place in Ferocia, a mythical country symbolizing the world as a whole, where Peter Cash reigns supreme. All the women are totally devoted to him and buy him whatever he wants, forcing their husbands to work more and more so that they can satisfy his needs—hence the double meaning of the "Horns of Plenty" in the subtitle. An enterprising visitor to Ferocia, Thomas Proctor, sees an opportunity for profit in this syndrome and makes a fortune by manufacturing and selling whatever Peter Cash happens to demand of the deluded women. After a while, however, Cash's demands become so arbitrary and capricious that Proctor and his partners are faced with ruin, since they have large stocks of newly manufactured articles on hand that they cannot get rid of because Peter Cash keeps changing his mind as to what he wants. Several businessmen, indeed, commit suicide because they have followed Proctor's lead with less precautions and foresight than he has brought to the affair, and they are consequently completely ruined. Free enterprise has failed, the stock market has crashed, and it is time for a controlled economy to come in. Pérez Dann puts this in dramatic terms by having Proctor take Cash in hand and order him to demand those articles that have already been manufactured. In this way Proctor, by manipulating the market, is always ahead of the game because he can decree what the demand will be before he creates the supply. At the end of the play Peter Cash is totally enslaved, although forced to proclaim that he is free; and Proctor and his associates are in complete control. Though the play is too long and the symbolism of the character of Peter Cash tends to become somewhat blurred, Pérez Dann has created a thoroughly dramatic tour-de-force in this panoramic survey of economic history in theatrical terms. If he fails to follow up his talent, it will be another black mark against the Spanish censorship.

Although there has inevitably been a sharp curtailment of foreign influences on Spanish theater practice, most of the popular—and permitted—plays of the commercial theater, such as the works of Alfonso Paso and Miguel Mihura, seem both in form and content as if they had stepped out of the 1920's just as if nothing at all had happened in between. However, two outside influences in particular are frequently discernible. One of these is Brecht, whose style, if not his politics—the philosophy of Communism is without influence even among those most strenuously opposed to the incumbent government—is profoundly admired by the new playwrights. The other is Erwin Piscator, who also, of course, had a marked influence on Brecht himself. Piscator was the first director to make effective and widespread use of other media in the theater. He visited Barcelona in 1937, and his influence is still important in the underground theater.[3]

The influence of both Brecht and Piscator can clearly be seen in the experiments that Alberto Miralles, a young teacher at the Instituto de Teatro in Barcelona, initiated in 1967 with a group of his students. Calling themselves the *Cátaro* group, they decided to try to create plays by dramatizing the ideas that came to them in discussions and in improvised rehearsals. The result, although Miralles was sufficiently in control as director and coordinator of the discussions to qualify as the author in the sense of being the guiding and unifying spirit, was essentially a communal effort. Their first creation was *Espectáculo Cátaro* ("*Cátaro* Spectacle," 1967), subtitled *El hombre y la guerra* ("Man and War"). This, as might be expected from a communal creation, is excessively simplistic. When all the members of a group have to be ideologically satisfied with an effort, even though they may be in basic agreement philosophically, nuances of thought are inevitably ironed out and we get a play that consists of obvious contrasts between ideal morality and practice. Although the principal influences on the style of the spectacle are clearly Brecht and Piscator, it resembles more the fervent and oversimplified evangelism of contemporary American "street" or "guerrilla" theatre in its thought. This is not to deny that there are some excellent scenes in it, such as the one contrasting various religious beliefs and the confusion they create in men's minds, but on the whole the spectacle is another example of a sermon that can affect only the already converted. The same cannot be said of the *Cátaro* group's third spectacle, *Catarocolón* ("Cataro-Columbus," 1968).[4] Here the skillful guiding hand of Miralles is more distinctly in evidence and we have a superbly written historical play. Historical plays used to be animated schoolroom lectures, usually with a patriotic view to glorifying the past. In our times they have become vehicles for the re-interpretation of history, with the cynical and more accurate purpose of debunking the "glorious" past and showing that it was no more morally exalted than the sordid present. Columbus and Luther have been among the most prominent candidates for re-interpretation. Washington, Lincoln, and Christ wait in the wings for enterprising new playwrights. The re-interpretation that Miralles and the *Cátaro* group give us in this play is Columbus as the quintessentially artful and devious schemer instead of Columbus the idealist. The reason that he finds it necessary to bring all his deviousness to bear is that late fifteenth century Spain, the period of the Catholic Monarchs glorified in all the official Spanish history books, is shown as completely corrupt, cynical, and concerned exclusively with business hypocritically disguised as religion. Their

Catholic Majesties are depicted as nothing more or less than the chief executives of an enormous commercial enterprise, concerned solely with beating their principal business competitors, the Portuguese, to whatever booty may be wrested from the new continent. It is interesting to contrast this play with Jura Soyfer's *Christopher Columbus* and with the play of the same name by Kurt Tucholsky and Walter Hasenclever.[5] In these two plays there is the same cynical depiction of the expedition and its discovery, but the focus is on the modern United States, the result of these sordid beginnings, which are used as a partial explanation of its present lamentable state. In Miralles' play the focus is on modern Spain with the same object in view.

The production history of *Catarocolón* also casts an interesting sidelight on one thorny aspect of that modern Spain—the censorship. As might be expected, the play was banned, but when it was re-submitted with the title "Minor Verses for an Illustrious Man" it was permitted and won the Guipúzcoa Prize for 1968. Under whatever title it may be presented, however, the play demonstrates that Alberto Miralles is a gifted all round theater man and an incisive thinker able to cast his thoughts into effective dramatic form.

Several other dramatists deserve mention for their attempts to overcome the obstacles facing them as writers in Spain today. These are men who have not yet reached the full development of their abilities but who have shown that they have the potential to join the ranks of the dramatists previously examined in this study.

Julio López Medina, who makes his home in Valladolid, has been writing since 1955, although his productivity is not nearly as great as that of Antonio Martínez Ballesteros, the playwright whose work his plays resemble most. Medina has recently written *Dadá, Gogó y Mas*, an amusing short play in which two men of diametrically opposed views on art and life get into a violent argument at a far-out modern art exhibition, but since both of them turn out to be stone deaf, nothing is resolved. Not only does their argument fail to leave them any the wiser: they do not even realize that they have been arguing. A more mature play is the full length *Un señor cualquiera* ("Mr. Anybody"), in which Medina uses the office metaphor for life that we have found previously in Ballesteros' *Los mendigos* and *El pensamiento circular* and in Quiles' *El asalariado*. Indeed, Medina's play is extraordinarily similar to these in its depiction of an office employee's emasculation by the system from which he cannot escape. Medina shows a sensitive feeling for the emotions of his anonymous protagonist in this play without in any way descending to sentimentalism.

Luis Riaza has recently attracted some attention in underground circles with *Las jaulas* ("The Cages"), a transposition of the Oedipus myth and its sequels to modern times. The play is divided into three parts dealing successively with Oedipus, the Seven against Thebes, and Antigone. This is very much a technically experimental play; so much so, indeed, that the meaning tends to become subordinated to the virtuosity of the construction. Riaza uses a play within a play framework with the actors taking turns assuming different roles by means of masks and costume changes in full view of the audience. The title derives from the fact that the platform on which the action of the play within the play takes place is ringed with cages containing chickens which are killed one by one during the course of the drama as a symbolic parallel to the deaths of the characters in the legend.

Riaza is clearly a talented writer who has not yet found his style. In this he is similar to Hermógenes Saínz, whose *La madre* ("The Mother") is a political allegory. Two enormous puppets act out the moves with which the Great Powers threaten the individual struggling to survive as something other than a pawn in the Great Political Power Game. This latter group is represented by a mother and her feeble-minded son whom she strives to protect at all costs, giving birth to an atom bomb to do so. Here again, as with Riaza, imagination triumphs over clarity, but there is promise for the future and it needs only encouragement to develop.

Another name that has recently emerged is that of Alfonso Jiménez Romero, a young teacher in a small town near Seville, whose *Oratorio* received one of the numerous provincial drama prizes in 1968. *Oratorio* was performed in the streets of Lebrija and subsequently taken to the Nancy Festival of Drama in France. It is a recreation of a folk play suitable for presentation by non-professionals. The Antigone legend and the story of Cain and Abel, among others, are used as the material for poetic, chanted incantations on the freedom of the human spirit. Jiménez has more recently turned to experimentation with surrealist technique in *El inmortal* ("The Immortal").[6]

There are many authors that have not been touched upon in this brief survey of the resurgence of the Spanish theater. Some, like

SPANISH UNDERGROUND DRAMA

Antonio Buero-Vallejo, Alfonso Sastre, Carlos Muñiz, and Lauro Olmo, are already known through publication in the United States and through the writings of other critics; some still remain to be discovered. Others, such as Francisco Nieva, Spain's leading scene designer, have concentrated less on political theater than on imaginative fantasies.[7] The future of the Spanish theater lies with these playwrights. The attempt to suppress them is futile. Their works exist and will inevitably be recognized as the continuation of the great theatrical tradition of Spain. No stronger or more reasoned warning against the evil inherent in the hubristic practice of censorship has ever been written than John Milton's in *Areopagitica*: "revolutions of ages do not oft recover the loss of a rejected truth, for the want of which whole nations fare the worse. We should be wary therefore what persecution we raise against the living labors of public men, how we spill that seasoned life of man perserved and stored up in books; since we see a kind of homicide may be thus committed [of] . . . the birth of reason itself . . ." No fitter words could be found to close this book.

NOTES

1. The text of this play was published in *Primer Acto*, No. 118, March, 1970.

2. *Mi guerra* was published in *Primer Acto*, No. 80, 1966; *El insaciable Peter Cash* was published in part in *Primer Acto*, Nos. 123–124, 1970.

3. Xavier Fábregas, *Teatre Català d'agitació política* (Barcelona: Edicions 62, 1969), p. 253.

4. I have not been able to obtain a copy of the second spectacle; *Catarocolón* was published in *Primer Acto*, No. 104, 1969.

5. Cf. the translation of the latter in *German Drama Between the Wars* ed. by George Wellwarth (New York: E. P. Dutton & Co., 1972) and the study of the former by the present writer in *American-German Review*, XXXV, iii (1969), 22–26.

6. Jiménez' latest plays, *Conversaciones con un niño* ("Conversations With a Child") and *Oración de la Tierra* ("Earth Prayer"), were not available in time for inclusion in this study.

7. Nieva has written *Tórtolas, crepúsculo . . . y telón* ("Turtledoves, Shadow . . . and Curtain"), an extremely ingenious Pirandellian play on illusion and reality; *Es bueno no tener cabeza* ("It's Nice Not To Have a Head"), a one-act farce that has had some success in production, is set in the

Middle Ages and involves a hilarious exchange of heads and sex among some alchemists; *Malditas sean Coronado y sus hijos* ("Accursed Be Coronado and His Children"), *El corazón acelerado* ("The Accelerated Heart"), and *Lord Bashaville*, a take-off on Oscar Wilde.

INDEX